Library of
Davidson College

ITALY, NATO, AND THE EUROPEAN COMMUNITY
The Interplay of Foreign Policy and Domestic Politics

HARVARD STUDIES IN INTERNATIONAL AFFAIRS
Number 31

ITALY, NATO, AND THE EUROPEAN COMMUNITY
The Interplay of Foreign Policy and Domestic Politics

By *Primo Vannicelli*

FOREWORD
By
Stanley Hoffmann

Published by the
Center for International Affairs
Harvard University

Copyright © 1974 by the President and Fellows of Harvard College
Library of Congress Catalog Card Number 74–79017
ISBN 0–87674–026–3

Printed in the United States of America

The Center is happy to provide a forum for the expression of responsible views. It does not however necessarily agree with those views.

Harvard University
Center for International Affairs
Executive Committee

RAYMOND VERNON, Herbert F. Johnson Professor of International Business Management, Director
SAMUEL P. HUNTINGTON, Frank G. Thomson Professor of Government, Associate Director
ROBERT R. BOWIE, Clarence Dillon Professor of International Affairs
DANIEL BELL, Professor of Sociology
PAUL M. DOTY, Mallinckrodt Professor of Biochemistry
LESTER E. GORDON, Director of the Harvard Institute for International Development
STANLEY HOFFMANN, Professor of Government
SEYMOUR MARTIN LIPSET, Professor of Government and Sociology
JOSEPH S. NYE, JR., Professor of Government
EDWIN O. REISCHAUER, University Professor
THOMAS C. SCHELLING, Lucius N. Littauer Professor of Political Economy
SIDNEY VERBA, Professor of Government

Created in 1958, the Center for International Affairs fosters advanced study of basic world problems by scholars from various disciplines and senior officials from many countries. The research of the Center focuses on economic, social, and political development; the management of force in the modern world; the problems and relations of advanced industrial societies; transnational processes and international order; and technology and international affairs.

The Harvard Studies in International Affairs, which are listed at the back of this book, may be ordered from the Publications Office, Center for International Affairs, 6 Divinity Avenue, Cambridge, Mass. 02138, at the prices indicated. Recent books written under the auspices of the Center, listed on the last pages, may be obtained from bookstores or ordered directly from the publishers.

ABOUT THE AUTHOR

Primo Vannicelli received his Ph.D. from Harvard University in 1970 and from 1971–1973 was a Research Fellow at the Harvard Center for International Affairs. Since 1970 he has been on the faculty of the Department of Politics at the University of Massachusetts-Boston, where he is currently an Assistant Professor and an Associate Dean.

Contents

Abbreviations	viii
Foreword by Stanley Hoffmann	ix
Introduction	1
1. Italian Political Responses to NATO and the EEC	4
NATO's Impact on Domestic Politics, 1948–49	5
The Treaty of Rome and the Political Parties, 1957	9
2. Political Significance of the EEC and NATO	16
Dynamics of Internalization	20
NATO as a Political Context	22
3. Italy's Behavior Towards the European Community	28
Integrative Behavior at the Domestic Level	29
Integrative Behavior at the EEC Level	42
4. Conclusion: European Unification or Atlantic Solidarity?	47
Notes	53

ABBREVIATIONS

COMECON	— Communist Council for Mutual Economic Assistance
CGIL	— Confederazione Generale Italiana del Lavoro (Communist-dominated labor confederation)
DC	— Democrazia Cristiana (Christian Democratic party)
ECSC	— European Coal and Steel Community
EDC	— European Defense Community
EEC	— European Economic Community
EFTA	— European Free Trade Area
FEOGA	— EEC Agricultural Fund
MLF	— Multilateral Nuclear Force
MSI	— Movimento Sociale Italiano (Neo-Fascist party)
NATO	— North Atlantic Treaty Organization
OEEC	— Organization for European Economic Cooperation
PCI	— Partito Comunista Italiano (Communist party)
PLI	— Partito Liberale Italiano (a small conservative party)
PRI	— Partito Repubblicano Italiano (a moderate conservative party)
PSDI	— Partito Socialista Democratico Italiano (Social Democratic party)
PSI	— Partito Socialista Italiano (Nenni's Socialist party)
PSIUP	— Partito Socialista Unità Proletaria (Left-wing Socialist party, organized in 1964)
PSLI	— (Social Democratic party; this name was used between 1947 and 1951, when it was changed to PSDI)

FOREWORD
BY STANLEY HOFFMANN

Primo Vannicelli's study is a major contribution to our understanding of Italian foreign policy as well as of Italy's domestic politics. The foreign policies of Italy's main partners in the European Community — France, West Germany, and England — have been scrutinized by scholars and commentators galore. Italy has been relatively neglected. Mr. Vannicelli's analysis provides both a remedy and an explanation. He shows that Italy's "choices of civilization," made in the early years of the cold war — membership in the Atlantic Alliance and participation in the West European enterprise — have remained the foundations of Italian foreign policy for a quarter of a century. But he also shows that these choices, far from creating, so to speak, a vehicle for a dynamic *foreign* policy, have instead served to build a shelter in which Italy would enjoy, at minimum cost, security and the economic benefits of European integration, and be allowed to concentrate on *domestic* tasks and politics. Choices which, for her three partners, were the condition or framework for regaining status and influence, meant a buffer between Italy and the storms of the world scene.

An active foreign policy was, for Bonn, a necessity; for London and Paris, a mixture of necessity and deliberate decision. Italy, deprived by World War II of colonial headaches, and otherwise comparatively intact, was not pushed onto the world stage by any cause or necessity, and chose to remain backstage. As Mr. Vannicelli indicates, a price had to be paid for that choice: Italy has probably derived from the Common Market fewer advantages than countries — such as France — that decided to fight for the prevalence of their interests within EEC with maximum aggressiveness. And Italy's voice in NATO has rarely been heard. But any alternative course of action — any active foreign policy, whether waged within the two communities joined by Italy or, as in the case of de Gaulle's France, at the expense of integration, might have had far greater disadvantages: first, because the terrain was already occupied by Italy's partners anyhow, secondly, because of the likely repercussion on domestic affairs.

Here we come to the most original part of Mr. Vannicelli's study. He shows that the foreign policy choices of Italy were above all geared to, and shaped, by the domestic scene. Here is a country that has been governed uninterruptedly for twenty-five years by the Christian Democrats (alone or with smaller allies). The two basic choices of Italian *foreign* policy started as a means of establishing within Italy a certain kind of political majority — a way of keeping out of power those who, on the far Right and (above all) on the Left and far Left, did not accept those choices. Later, they became a means of keeping the Center in power, a criterion for selecting the allies of the Christian Democrats, and a brake on any radical shift in power. By making the test of the "aptitude to govern" a foreign policy test, the Italian political system cleverly defused domestic tensions, since it shifted the vocabulary of politics from explosive internal issues to rather Byzantine external ones.

In other words, foreign policy issues in Italy are essentially symbolic, and refer to underlying domestic problems. We are dealing with a coded language, in which references to NATO or supranationality really have to be translated into domestic calculations and intrigues, and in which the latter, in turn, are disguised in frequently grandiloquent foreign policy schemes. The acceptance of a limited role in the world means the deliberate choice, and indeed the imposition, of limits within which governing coalitions can be formed. It thus becomes clear why the Communist party itself, in its glacial evolution toward a role in government, "signals" its internal shifts in foreign policy language (for instance, by letting it be known that it would not ask Italy to leave NATO). We are far beyond that point familiar to specialists of "linkages" between domestic and foreign affairs: the existence of important internal functions of a nation's foreign policy. We are practically at the point where the latter's main functions are domestic, or, to put it perhaps more fairly, where foreign policy is minimal and largely symbolic precisely for domestic purposes, and where foreign policy changes (consisting in nuances rather than abrupt turns) are made less because of external conditions than for internal reasons.

Mr. Vannicelli shows that Italy's presence in NATO and the EEC has tended to become an excuse for Italy's absence as a driving force on the world stage. On the whole, he refrains from judging the impact that Italy's often more verbal than committed support of NATO and EEC integration has made on these organizations. He also leaves open the question of whether the use of foreign policy for domestic "pattern maintenance" has been profitable to the Italian polity. Every reader will have to decide for himself, but he must be grateful to Mr. Vannicelli for having put all the elements for an evaluation at his disposal.

Introduction

> The traditional subdivisions of political science are such that . . . students of comparative politics tend to take the international environment for granted, as if national systems were immune to external influences and have full control over their own destinies. Similarly, students of international politics tend to make a series of simplifying assumptions about the international behavior of national systems, as if all such systems reacted in the same way to the same stimuli . . . The political unit is simply assumed to have an environment to which it responds and with which it interacts. Students of foreign policy examine the responses and students of international relations investigate the interactions, but neither group considers how the functioning of the unit itself is conditioned and affected by these responses and interactions.
>
> James Rosenau [1]

As a result of interdependence, intensity of communications, and membership in international organizations, most countries today cannot be regarded as distinct and insulated political units. They are more accurately described by the term "penetrated system," which implies the fusion of national and international factors. Although external pressures on domestic political institutions and processes have always existed, since 1945 there has been a significant proliferation of such pressures through numerous organizations which serve to institutionalize the process of penetration. This is hardly an original observation; but like much that is obvious, its meaning is not necessarily clear. The relationship between domestic politics and foreign policy has become so complex that categorization by existing schemes of analysis is no longer adequate. The mix becomes even more elusive when a country assumes commitments to various international organizations whose integrative pressures it can only partially control, and whose repercussions on domestic politics are neither clearly understood nor foreseeable. Although the various theories of international organization and integration have pointed to important aspects of this situation, they have yet to explain the full range of developments that are related directly or indirectly to the processes affecting a penetrated system.[2]

In the EEC case, Community considerations have influenced important areas of national policy-making; interest groups have partially shifted their expectations and demands to the Community level; the European Commission — the executive of the EEC — plays an important supranational role; national political elites are forced to give serious consideration to the regional organization in their political and economic actions; and there is widespread support for the regional idea, accompanied by a general perception of integration as beneficial. There is disagreement in the literature on European integration as to the extent of the impact that the regional process has had on national politics; but it is generally assumed that the EEC institutions play a crucial role in the internal politics of the member states.[3] Turning to the Atlantic Alliance, most of the literature has dealt with NATO either as a military alliance or in terms of general European-American relations; very limited attention has been given to the part that the Atlantic relationship plays domestically within each country, and how it has affected attitudes towards European unification.[4]

Nevertheless, since most of the studies of Europe have been based on the premise of the EEC as a developing community, in the early 1960s there was a tendency to envisage continuous progress towards regional unification. Yet it is ultimately at the national level that the future of regional integration will be determined. And in fact, in the late 1960s, the literature on European integration suggested that there were two important variables that had been underestimated in previous theories on the subjects: (1) the role of differing national political systems; (2) the impact of events outside the EEC.[5] Even more critical, perhaps, is the interaction between these two variables, as well as between each of them and the development of the EEC. Thus many basic questions remain to be explored. For example, how does a country's membership in two partly overlapping organizations, such as NATO and the EEC, affect its foreign and domestic policy? How does this in turn affect that country's behavior towards regional unification, as well as its response to integrative pressures? How do these regional and extra-regional pressures interact with a changing domestic political scene?

Several studies are now available on most facets of Italian national politics, of Italian foreign policy, and of the influence of domestic politics on foreign policy. But no analysis exists of the impact of the EEC on Italy or of Italy's responses domestically and within the European Community. Except for very general references to Italy in studies on the EEC from a systemic point of view, the literature that deals specifically with Italy and European unification consists of either vague and partisan tracts or specialized legal and economic analyses. On the other hand, an extensive literature exists on NATO; but it either discusses the military aspects of the alliance or presents polemical arguments for and against Italy's presence in it.[6] The two fundamental themes of Italian foreign and domestic policy in the postwar period — European unity and Atlantic Alliance — still have to be examined in relation to their impact on Italy's domestic and regional behavior.

The purpose of this monograph is to analyze the relationships between Italy's Atlantic orientation, its commitment to European unification, and its domestic politics — with regard to Italy's integrative behavior, nationally and within the European Community, that results from these interactions and from the dynamics of its political system. The conceptual framework of this study derives from the theory of regional integration in general and the literature on European unification in particular. Thus many of the conclusions presented here provide a testing ground for some of the major assumptions in the theoretical literature. This study also highlights certain political dynamics that may help develop a more comprehensive analytic framework for penetrated systems.

It is with pleasure that I acknowledge my gratitude to Harvard University's Professor Stanley Hoffmann, *maestro di color che sanno*, for his good-humored guidance and encouragement; and to Professors Joseph S. Nye, Jr. and Samuel H. Beer, also of Harvard University, for their many helpful suggestions. I also received invaluable assistance from Mrs. Dorothy Whitney and Mr. Peter Jacobsohn, former and present Editor of Publications of the Center for International Affairs at Harvard University. I am very grateful to the CFIA, to the Center for European Studies, and to the University of Massachusetts at Boston for helping to make this publication possible.

And special thanks to Marsha, whose presence made the difference.

1. Italian Political Responses to NATO and the EEC

Political parties play a preponderant role in every phase of Italian politics. They form the center of activity for the government, the interest groups, and all other significant political forces in the country. Major policy decisions as well as the making and unmaking of governments have been transferred from parliament to the party oligarchies. Although a similar trend can be noted in other countries, this development has reached a well-nigh pathological level in Italy with the result that the fractionalizing of the electorate and the ideological divisions among various parties prevent the emergence of stable and effective governments. Since 1948, the Italian political system has in effect been deadlocked between the dominant governing party (Christian Democrats) and the dominant opposition party (Communists), which together have consistently received about 65 percent of the vote. Other parties could only aspire to a share of power by participating in a coalition government with either of these two parties.[7]

This situation also reflects the country's social environment. In fact, in most democratic states, "the role which the political system plays is to a large extent determined by the economic and social structure of the nation, and by the values of the main social groups."[8] The Christian Democrats (DC) and the Communist party (PCI) have been able to exert a polarizing and stalemating impact on the Italian political system because they are the political expression of Catholicism and Marxism — two traditions with deep-seated roots in Italy which in effect constitute the core of the country's two major subcultures. The DC and the PCI also control the vast majority of labor unions, most of the social and cultural community agencies, and most of the local governments. Because these two parties are also the two largest political employers their pervasive role has been reinforced by numerous pragmatic interests which in turn have deepened their cohesion. All other parties, caught between the polarizing attraction of the two major parties and traditions, have experienced divisions and severe internal controversies which have further reduced their effectiveness.

Given the permanence of the DC in the leadership of every government, the inevitable result has been the emergence of strong factions within the party. The struggle for power in the system has been reflected in factional struggles within the DC, and the consolidation of the party's dominant role has brought about a parallel crystallization of its factions. But, checked by a common ideological allegiance and above all by a concrete interest in wishing to remain the major government party, the warring DC factions have always stopped short of creating actual party schisms. At the same time, over the years, as majority control within the DC oligarchy has shifted from one faction to another, most governmental crises have in effect resulted from those shifts rather than from conflicts among various parties. Having assumed extraordinary political importance, the DC factions have been courted and influenced by other parties and thus have also contributed to the stalemating tendencies of the political system.

In addition, given the non-consensual nature of Italian society and the irreconcilable divisions in the structure of the political system, the parties have tended to transform parliament into an arena for ideological confrontation. Thus, in the postwar period, there has been an abundance of rhetoric and uncompromising debate in the Italian political system, but a striking inability to produce consistent policy and long-range plans. As a result, international developments have exerted a pervasive impact on domestic politics.

NATO's Impact on Domestic Politics, 1948–49

A heated debate accompanied Italy's acceptance of the NATO treaty in March 1949. For several months before the signing of the treaty, representatives of every political opinion vehemently expressed their views in Parliament and elsewhere; Socialists and Communists engaged in filibustering against the treaty; violent riots and demonstrations took place in many cities. The outcome of the confrontation was known in advance: the government was assured of a comfortable majority in Parliament. Yet the debate continued to rage even after Italy's formal acceptance of the treaty because, in effect, the shape of Italy's postwar political system was being determined in conjunction with the NATO decision in 1948–49. Two fundamentally conflicting visions of the political system were reflected in the parties' response to the NATO treaty: in favor of the alliance were those factions and parties that accepted the prospect of a conservative system dominated by the Christian Democrats; opposed were those that wanted radical alternatives. Italy's decision to join NATO, while not the direct cause of this rift, helped transform the politically still fluid situation in 1948 into a stalemate in which all parties were classified into two tight categories along cold war lines.[9] This ended all possibility of a dialogue among some important political groups, particularly between the Socialist parties and the Christian Democrats.

The views expressed by Christian Democratic spokesmen during the parliamentary debates on the NATO treaty paralleled the official government line. Joining the alliance was presented as a choice of civilization — "scelta di civiltà." They argued that Italy could not safely remain neutral; that NATO would provide security and promote the country's reemergence as an independent nation. Although the speeches of the various DC leaders gave the impression of solid unanimity, a significant internal debate was taking place within the party; and the publications of the leftist factions of the DC openly expressed those conflicts. The DC Left played strongly on the theme of European unity — which by then had also become an explicit commitment of the DC and the Italian government — arguing that adherence to NATO would undermine all chances of European unification.

As an alternative to the Atlantic Alliance, the DC Left advocated a unified Europe that would play a mediatory role between the USA and the USSR and could thus help prevent the division of the world into blocs. The DC Left was convinced that only a government based on the cooperation of all political forces could succeed in modernizing Italy's economic and social structures. And, in view of the foreign policy espoused by the Socialists and Communists, it regarded a neutralist foreign policy as essential to prevent a split between the government parties and the opposition. Correctly, as it turned out, the DC Left feared that a polarization between Communists and anti-Communists on the international scene as a result of the creation of NATO would bring about a similar development within Italy.[10] The creation of the Atlantic Alliance and Italy's decision to join it did indeed prevent the DC from moving left. For in choosing NATO, the DC majority was not engaging in a simple act of foreign policy-making: the way in which the decision was arrived at, as well as its repercussions, amounted to a definition of the party's domestic orientation. Against these developments of 1948–49 it is possible to understand the meaning of subsequent criticism of NATO by the DC Left. Within the Christian Democratic party, as well as within the political system in general, NATO was to remain a symbol to which the party periodically reaffirmed its "fidelity." It was also the symbol of the various forces, within and without the party, that were seeking a new leftist domestic policy.

A similar controversy, with similar results, took place within the Social Democratic party (PSDI). In December 1947, having split from the Socialist Party (Pietro Nenni's PSI), the Social Democrats joined the government to prevent the DC from forming a coalition with right-wing parties. But the NATO issue caught the party in a serious dilemma. On the one hand, it could not oppose the government and DC position on NATO for fear of a split in the coalition cabinet, which would probably have resulted in a turn to the right. On the other hand, acceptance of NATO conflicted with the party's rejection of military blocs. Above all, it conflicted with the party's hope that, as an alternative to both Communism and Christian Democracy, cooperation among all socialist groups and parties was still possible. In short, the Social Democrats feared that acceptance of NATO would make their break with the Nenni Socialists final, and would thus remove the possibility of cooperation with other socialist forces that were also opposed to military alliances. Like the DC Left, this group was concerned primarily with the domestic effect of NATO: that it would compel the various political forces within Italy to form two rigid blocs. Although aware of this prospect, the majority wing of the party under Giuseppe Saragat hoped that ultimately NATO would be a guarantee against the seizure of power by either the extreme Left or the extreme Right.

The bitter debate that developed within the Social Democratic party on the NATO issue was not resolved by the leaders' decision to allow individual deputies to vote according to their conscience on the Atlantic Treaty. The Saragat wing succeeded in keeping the party in the coalition government, and thus accepted NATO, even if reluctantly. This was soon to have a damaging effect on the Social Democratic party. In 1949 there still were several loosely-organized groups of social democratic orientation, within and without Nenni's Socialist party, which could have been rallied to merge into the Social Democratic party and thus enhance its electoral appeal as well as its influence within the coalition government. During that year, an autonomous group of moderate socialists (organized around Ignazio Silone) and a large faction within the Socialist party (organized around Giuseppe Romita) attempted to merge into the Social Democratic party. But the efforts at unification failed because the Silone and the Romita groups, although both social democratic in domestic orientation, were firmly committed to a neutralist foreign policy and could not accept the Social Democratic party's commitment to NATO.[11]

Italy's acceptance of NATO was to have an even greater impact on Nenni's Socialist party. That party's intense campaign of opposition to NATO, before and after the ratification of the treaty in 1949, has been regarded as evidence of the Socialists' subjection to the Communist party (PCI) during the first postwar decade. But the electoral agreement between the two parties — the Popular Front — had in fact been terminated by August 1948, following the victory of the Socialist party's moderate wing at the June 1948 party congress. The party's continued neutralism in foreign policy derived from socialist ideology and tradition; it was not a mere echo of the Communist pro-Soviet line. In addition, the party was opposed to NATO because it believed that Italy's membership in the alliance would shift the domestic political balance to the right.

The Socialists were obsessed with two interrelated issues: the unity of the working class (and hence the problem of the party's relations with the PCI) and, secondly, a pervasive fear that without a united working class the conservative parties and their backers would prevail and gradually reintroduce a reactionary system. Haunted by the belief that the victory of fascism in 1919–22 was directly related to the split in the working-class parties, the Socialists could not favor any international development that might contribute to a polarization of Italian politics. Thus the Socialist party for years continued to oppose NATO — as long as the hope remained that the working-class parties would cooperate in providing an alternative to a regime dominated by the Christian Democrats. For the Socialists to accept NATO in 1949 would have meant a severe rift in their relations with the PCI, and also a split within the labor movement. On the other hand, the Socialists' opposition to NATO enabled the conservative groups within the government parties to succeed in relegating the leftist parties to a position of sterile alienation.[12]

NATO's impact on the socialist movement was enormously pervasive and destructive. After emerging from the 1947 split of the Socialist party, Saragat's Social Democratic party had by 1948 decided to work within the existing system and to participate in a coalition government with more conservative parties. While critical of the Socialists for collaborating with the PCI, the Social Democrats refused to take an anti-Communist stand. And although they believed in the necessity of a tactical alliance with the PCI, the Socialists had not subordinated their ideological vision and their commitment to the democratic method to Soviet and PCI interests. In other words, while the differences between the Socialists and the Social Democrats were profound, the possibility of cooperation and reconciliation still existed prior to the NATO decision. (In the more relaxed atmosphere of the early 1960s the two parties were to collaborate in a coalition government and eventually were to be reunited into a single socialist party).

In early 1949, before the ratification of the NATO Treaty, the Socialist party was controlled by its moderate centrist faction, which was favorable to an entente with the Social Democrats. The incentive for such an entente was obvious: there was little likelihood that either the Socialists or the Social Democrats could individually obtain sufficient electoral support to provide an alternative to a government coalition controlled either by the DC or the PCI. A joint effort by all socialist groups and parties, however, offered such a possibility. Yet, because of the Socialists' commitment to a neutralist foreign policy, collaboration with the Social Democrats remained unattainable. Henceforth, the Atlantic Alliance was to symbolize and reinforce the disagreements between the two socialist parties.[13]

The elimination of any possibility of cooperation between the Social Democrats and the more powerful Socialist party also reduced the potential influence of the former within the coalition government. The victory of the Center-Right factions within the Christian Democratic party, which had been aided by the decision to join NATO, further reduced the influence of the Social Democrats. The result was that the political parties in power rejected the notion of alliances with the Left but maintained an "opening to the Right" for over a decade.

Internationally, Italy's postwar position — inferior and isolated, like Germany's — improved as a result of membership in NATO. Domestically, the widespread sense of insecurity was also relieved. Through the 1950s and 1960s, groups favoring the status quo continued to believe that Italy's membership in NATO was essential to the country's stability. On the other hand, reformist groups (left-wing parties, as well as leftist factions within the DC) came to regard the Atlantic Alliance as a fundamental obstacle to change. The result was a self-fulfilling prophecy: by becoming a symbol of domestic divisions, NATO also contributed to their aggravation and rigidity. As a consequence, since 1949 the domestic controversy over the orientation of the political system was to be consistently linked with the debate on the validity of the Atlantic relationship.

THE TREATY OF ROME AND THE POLITICAL PARTIES, 1957

Many of the political dynamics that characterized Italy's entry into the Atlantic Alliance came into play again during 1957 in conjunction with the ratification of the Treaty of Rome which established the European Economic Community. The political parties extensively debated regional integration. More than a decade was to pass before another comprehensive evaluation would be made of the substance, problems, and aims of European unification. During that decade discussions consisted merely of either vague reaffirmations of the views presented in 1957 or expressions of interest in specific economic problems. The 1957 debates provide a picture of three basic attitudes of the various parties towards the European Community:

(1) Total support for political and economic integration as a part of the Atlantic system by the Christian Democrats, Social Democrats, the conservative Liberals (PLI), and Republicans (PRI).
(2) Positive attitude towards integration, but primary interest in promoting a socialistic and autonomous Europe by the Socialists.
(3) Opposition to integration as envisaged in the Treaty of Rome by the Communists.

Although some changes occurred within the last two categories in later years, the basic attitudes remained the same.

By the early 1950s, as shown by their response to the European Coal and Steel Community (ECSC), the Christian Democrats, Liberals, Republicans, and Social Democrats were fully committed to the goal of economic and political integration in Europe. All Italian governments consistently adopted a similar attitude, even against the opposition of industrial groups, as in the case of the ECSC. During 1957 and since, the position of every Italian government has been based on three assumptions. First, as will be shown, the regional process in Europe has been linked to the NATO alliance; Italy's commitment to Atlantic solidarity and European unity is perceived as indivisible, and the two processes are regarded as mutually reinforcing. Second, economic integration is regarded as an almost automatic step towards political unification, which is seen as an essential goal. Third, a definite commitment has been made to an outward-looking Europe.

These assumptions are, of course, also those of the Christian Democratic party, the dominant partner in every postwar government. Its commitment to European unification has been regularly reaffirmed at virtually every meeting of the party's leadership since the early postwar period. During the 1957 debates on the Treaty of Rome, the DC spokesmen expressed firm support for a European Community with strong decision-making powers and with a single and powerful assembly. Criticism of the treaty was insignificant and merely aimed at urging the government to demand certain concessions favorable to specific economic interests that might be negatively affected by the removal of tariffs. Although no opposition to the Community emerged within the DC, a debate arose over the question of what kind of Europe the party should insist on: the left wing visualized an autonomous Europe, and was critical of the DC majority's goal of European unification as an integral part of the Atlantic system. Because these conflicting views formed part of intra-DC debates on the direction of domestic policy, they were never examined on their own merits; thus the potential incongruity between the goal of European unity and the commitment to Atlantic solidarity was never clearly perceived.[14]

The views of the Social Democrats resembled those of the government and the DC. In addition, the PSDI believed that the European Community should develop a common policy covering all economic sectors and that social legislation in various countries should be harmonized. The PSDI wanted the EEC to become an effective economic union capable of promoting the special interests of workers. In this sense, the PSDI believed with the PSI that European integration would advance the cause of the working class by transferring socialist efforts to a wider field. Within the restricted national arena, according to the Social Democrats, the DC and the PCI protracted the political stalemate by regarding each other as a serious threat; on the other hand, in the wider European context the PSDI hoped to collaborate with other socialist parties and thus to exert sufficient influence to resolve the national impasse.

Though varying in the degree of genuine commitment to regional integration and espousing different political and economic aims, the Center parties did provide a base of support for the government's policy towards the European Community. This base of support contained, however, some potential defects that were to affect the country's response to integration. Having assumed, almost as an act of faith, that NATO and the European Community were two mutually reinforcing institutions, these parties could be expected to oppose any developments in Europe that might reduce the solidity of the Atlantic relationship. In addition, the parties showed a certain inconsistency in their commitment to regional unification which later was to help produce incongruous policies.

With the exception of its left-wing minority, Nenni's Socialist party accepted European integration — in striking contrast to the Communists. Significantly, most of the PSI's polemics against the Treaty of Rome were actually a response to attacks by the PCI. However, the Socialists were opposed to the government's demand for four-year decree powers to implement the first phase of the treaty; they wanted to limit the delegation of powers to one year to insure parliamentary participation. They also objected to the government's maneuver which excluded the extreme Left from the election of representatives to the European Assembly. Despite these objections, the party did not change its position of benevolent abstention on the ratification vote. The objections, in fact, showed support for regional integration in that they were aimed at making the European Assembly genuinely representative and at assuring the continuing involvement of the Italian Parliament in implementing the Treaty of Rome.

Having decided, by 1957, to seek a Center-Left alliance with the

DC, the Socialists saw in the European Community an opportunity to gain support for their domestic policies; they expected the EEC to become the focus for united action by various labor unions; and they hoped that in preparation for the EEC challenges the DC and government leaders would have to initiate four-year plans and thereby become more receptive to the PSI's goal of large-scale domestic planning. On the other hand, the Socialists were aware of the potentially negative effects of the EEC on some segments of the Italian economy and on large sectors of the work force in particular. But unlike the PCI, instead of opposing integration for these reasons they actually demanded that the EEC expand its scope. Convinced that a mere customs union would not help resolve the structural problems of the Italian economy, the Socialists called for a genuine economic union and were critical of the Treaty of Rome for not insisting on full economic integration.

The Socialists were thus even more solidly in favor of economic integration than the government and the Center parties. Potential for disagreement existed, however, between the PSI and the Center parties over the political form the European Community was to assume. In contrast with the Center parties' view of the Community as directly linked to the Atlantic Alliance, the PSI was committed to the vision of an autonomous Europe as a way of eliminating the cold war blocs.[15] These conflicting viewpoints were to have important consequences in the 1960s when the simultaneous commitment to European unification and to the Atlantic relationship became untenable.

From the time plans for the European Community were first discussed in Italy in the early 1950s, the Communist party was caught between numerous conflicting pressures: the party's ideology, its domestic strategy, the Soviet position regarding European unification, the special needs of the CGIL (the Communist-dominated labor federation), and finally, the Socialist party's fluctuating relations with the government coalition. Consequently, beginning with the debates on the Treaty of Rome in 1957, the Communist position on the European Community was marked by a great deal of ambiguity. The party remained opposed to regional integration limited to Western Europe and oriented to the Atlantic Alliance; it also remained critical of the supranational features of the European Community and of the goal of political unification. In accord with the Soviet response to the Treaty of Rome, the PCI regarded the EEC (like OEEC, NATO, and ECSC before) as another manifestation of American imperialism, and as a "conspiracy of monopolists" against the workers and small producers. The PCI predicted that the EEC would have disastrous consequences for the working class, that it would undermine national sovereignty, and that it would adversely affect

East-West relations by favoring imperialistic and conservative interests.[16] Thus, despite some resemblance between the Communist and Socialist criticisms of the treaty, there was a fundamental difference in their policies. The PSI had accepted the prospect of European integration as a challenge which it would meet in a cooperative and constructive manner, domestically and at the EEC level. On the other hand, the PCI still defined its role as one of direct opposition to the existing political system and its international commitments.

Apart from the Communists, then, in 1957 most political parties were in favor of the European Community. However, two critical issues remained. First, potential disagreements cut across the various parties regarding the political purpose of a united Europe and its relationship with the USA. In the climate of 1957 this was not of great significance; but in subsequent years these disagreements reappeared and blended with the domestic debate over the political direction Italy was to take, thus affecting the ability of parties and governments to promote integration. Second, although the vast majority of parties and elites explicitly advocated European political and economic unification, their support did not guarantee subsequent action. In fact, as Communist attacks on the EEC diminished in the early 1960s, there was little incentive for the other parties to go beyond ritualistic affirmations of support based on the positive declarations of 1957. The parties provided a permissive consensus, but not a stimulus, for the government and Parliament to press for integration both domestically and at the EEC level.

Impact on the Political System. Debates on ratification of the Treaty of Rome in 1957 took place at a time when significant international and domestic events touched off new developments within the Italian political system. The salient international events were the NATO crisis following Suez and the turmoil in the Communist world in the aftermath of both the Hungarian uprising and the 20th Congress of the Soviet Communist Party. The domestic political scene was dominated by the conflict between the DC and the PSDI over the formation of a Center-Left coalition, the split between the Socialists and the Communists, and debates within the DC regarding these two developments. As the responses of various political elites to the international events merged with the controversy on domestic political alignments, the Treaty of Rome itself became part of the domestic struggle.

By 1957 a deep rift had developed within the Socialist party. While the party's moderate wing under Nenni had decided to seek cooperation with the center parties with the aim of forming a coalition government, the left wing remained opposed to loosening the party's ties with the Communists. But the turmoil in Eastern Europe and in the Soviet Union had convinced the moderate wing that the PSI should completely sever its ties with the PCI. Because of the Communist party's opposition to the European Community, the debates on the Treaty of Rome within the Socialist party also affected the continuing dispute on domestic politics. And this process was intensified by assertions of DC and PSDI leaders that they regarded the intra-PSI debate on the European Community as a significant indication of the party's attitude towards the Communists, and thus a test of its seriousness about a potential Center-Left coalition.

The confrontation over the Treaty of Rome within the Socialist party thus became particularly intense. Although the party had decided to abstain long before the ratification vote in Parliament, on the eve of the vote the left wing staged a vehement attack against the treaty. Claiming that the EEC would reinforce the NATO alliance, this faction concluded that the party's neutralist commitment demanded a negative vote — even though the Socialist vote on the treaty, whether abstention or negative, would not affect the outcome; the treaty was assured of passage by a safe margin. The dispute, then, was not so much over the merits of the treaty as over the symbolic significance of the party's abstention on the ratification vote: it would signify the first instance of a split between Socialists and Communists on a major issue since World War II. Having failed in this attempt, the left-wing faction tried again a year later. Claiming that the economic difficulties Italy experienced during 1958 were due to its membership in the EEC, left-wing spokesmen demanded that the party change its neutral position of 1957 to one of definite condemnation of the Treaty of Rome. Of course such a change would have no concrete consequences for European unification; the real purpose, once again, was to use the EEC issue to undermine the growing efforts, then under way within the PSI and other parties, to move towards a Center-Left entente.[17]

In a less prominent fashion the EEC also played a role in the intra-DC controversy on whether the party should retain a centrist orientation or move to the Left. The Christian Democratic right-wing factions, as well as the Liberal party, argued that the Treaty of Rome created a new obligation for the "democratic parties" (meaning the Center-Right coalition) to avoid overtures to the Left because, they maintained, the influence of the Socialists would work against the spirit and aims of the EEC. On the other hand, the left-wing factions insisted that only a Center-Left government could promote the type of economic policies that were urgently needed to prepare Italy for the challenge of the EEC. The Atlantic Alliance, too, was drawn into the debate. The right-wing factions and parties insisted that European integration be linked with the NATO alliance. But in doing so they were not responding to external pressures; because of the strong symbolic connection between the Atlantic relationship and the centrist position in domestic politics (dating back to 1949), emphasis on the importance of the NATO link by the right-wing groups was a way of discrediting the efforts of the DC left factions to form a Center-Left coalition with the Socialist party. The purpose was clear: they hoped to show that because of the Socialists' commitment to an autonomous Europe, a Center-Left entente could not be reconciled with Italy's "Atlantic fidelity." [18]

These developments also had an impact on the Communist party. The disagreement between the PCI and the majority faction of the PSI over the Treaty of Rome did not merely stem from a conflicting evaluation of European integration; it reflected their views of the role that leftist parties should play within the existing political situation. While by 1957 the Socialist party had decided to seek an entente with the Center parties, its left wing and the Communist party were still committed to frontal opposition to the system. The situation was made even more complex by the position of the leftist labor confederation (CGIL) towards regional integration. In contrast to the Communist party, CGIL leaders maintained that, despite many difficulties, in the long run the EEC process would be beneficial to the workers; hence they wanted representation for their union within the European institutions. Because of the strong presence of Socialists in the CGIL and the PCI's determination to avoid a break with the union, Communist leaders tried to minimize the differences between their views and those of the CGIL concerning the EEC.[19] But profound differences remained, and the EEC became a symbol and a cause of the growing division between the Communist party, the Socialists, and the CGIL.

The effects of the Treaty of Rome on internal political developments were not as devastating as those of NATO in 1949. Virtually all political forces, however, responded to the European Community as they had to the Atlantic Alliance; they regarded it mainly as an external factor to be utilized to promote certain domestic political aims. In the early postwar period, the Center-Left forces in Italy had looked to European federalism as a liberating process that would break the impasse in national politics by transferring the confrontation to a wider European context in which the appeal of both the Communists and the Center-Right would diminish.[20] But the regional integration process initiated by the Treaty of Rome in the late 1950s no longer held this promise. As the EEC was rapidly utilized by both right and left forces to influence domestic politics, instead of helping to dissolve the Italian political stalemate the EEC actually became part of it.

2. POLITICAL SIGNIFICANCE OF THE EEC AND NATO

On the basis of their frequently reiterated commitment to European unification one would expect Italian political parties to devote considerable attention to major developments related to the EEC. Since 1948, various parties have in fact shown great interest in world affairs; they have debated international issues at some length and have consistently tried to influence Italian foreign policy. In addition, they have always reacted to EEC-related developments which affected or were likely to affect specific domestic economic interests. Yet they have generally failed to respond to other EEC-level developments even when such developments had serious implications for the shape and future of the European Community. For example, they virtually ignored the Fouchet Plan of 1962, the 1963 French veto on Britain's admission to the EEC, and the EEC crisis of 1965-66, which involved some of the most critical issues of European regional unification.

The Fouchet Plan. During 1961-62, following President de Gaulle's proposals for the political union of Europe, the six members of the EEC engaged in intensive negotiations (named the "Fouchet Plan" negotiations after the chairman of the intergovernmental committee appointed in response to the French proposal). The sharp divergence of opinion among the Six that emerged during the Fouchet negotiations were symptomatic of the two major unresolved issues confronting the European Community: supranational vs. intergovernmental approach to regional integration, and autonomous vs. Atlantic Europe. In fact, the major issues at stake in the Fouchet negotiations were to lead to the failure of the discussion on Britain's admission to the EEC in the early 1960s, (and, in particular, to the 1963 French veto).[21] They also had a significant impact on the EEC crisis of 1965-66 and on the continuing problems besetting European unification for the rest of the decade.

All Italian parties had made strong commitments concerning these issues. With the exception of the PCI, all parties favored the supranational approach; and most of them were also firmly committed to an Atlantic Europe and to Britain's admission. Hence it would have been natural for the party elites to express concern about the failure of the Fouchet Plan negotiations in April 1962. One would have expected them to seek to influence the Italian Government's actions within the European Community, particularly since Italy's insistence on Britain's admission was regarded in the Italian press as a major factor leading to the failure of the Fouchet negotiations; in addition, various independent publications were noting at the time that by continuing to insist on Britain's entry Italy might cause a serious French reaction with deleterious consequences for the unification process.[22]

By the end of April, it became clear that a serious crisis was brewing within the European Community, a crisis in which Italy had been and might well go on playing a significant role. Yet there was no reaction by the parties either in Parliament or in the press. By contrast, issues raised at the Atlantic Council's meeting during the same period received immediate and widespread attention by all parties, even though this was an area in which Italy's position could be of little consequence.[23] During the second half of 1962, many important questions continued to haunt the EEC and many developments were taking place that conflicted with the European vision of most Italian parties. As indicated by commentaries in the independent Italian press, a serious reexamination of national positions within the EEC was urgently needed, and specific policy decisions had to be made by the governments of the Six. Throughout this period, while the party elites engaged in extensive foreign policy debates on NATO-related issues in Parliament and in the party press, they ignored the European Community as well as the Italian government's specific policies and potential responses.[24]

The 1963 French Veto. By the end of 1962, many of the underlying problems within the European Community had come into the open. In Italy, press reports were calling attention to the urgency of the EEC crisis and the need for reappraising Italy's position towards the Community.[25] The French veto on Britain's admission in January 1963 was to dramatize the tensions within the Community and to heighten the concern for its future. The Italian press gave wide coverage to the crisis that followed the French veto; its response was not, however, matched by significant political reactions of the various parties. In January as well as in the following months the parties' greatest concern, within Parliament and in the party press, was not with the EEC crisis but with the MLF (multilateral nuclear force) Plan.

The parties' attention remained focused on the MLF even during the parliamentary discussions that followed a presentation by the Foreign Minister in which he had explicitly given priority to EEC issues. Instead of trying to determine what role the Italian government intended to play within the EEC in the aftermath of the French veto, spokesmen of various parties merely vaguely affirmed their commitment to European unity and Britain's admission without critically examining the issues. (In contrast, for instance, the German parliament hotly debated the EEC crisis and the role that the government ought to play within the Community). On the few occasions when the Italian parties dealt specifically with the EEC crisis, the actual concern did not seem to be with the regional process itself. Rather, the EEC crisis was utilized by right-wing parties and right-wing factions within the DC to discredit the moves then under way to establish a Center-Left coalition — arguing that such a coalition would undermine the country's commitment to regional integration, and that in fact Italy's ineffectiveness within the European Community stemmed from the Socialist party's influence on the government.[26]

By the end of February 1963 a general mood of distrust and uncertainty was emerging within the European Community. This became evident during the meeting of the EEC Council of Ministers on February 26 that had been called to sign a new agreement on relations between the EEC and affiliated African states. Italy announced that it could not commit itself to the new agreement. This refusal was interpreted as an attempt to punish France for its veto on the British issue and was strongly criticized by the Italian press and in the European Parliament as an approach that would only aggravate the crisis. Obviously the Italian government was playing a very controversial role within the EEC which could have repercussions for future developments. Yet there was no party response, in Parliament or in the press. Similarly, the electoral programs of various parties during the 1963 national elections showed a marked contrast between NATO issues and EEC problems: while the first were given extensive coverage, the second received only ritualistic assertions of support for European unity.[27]

The EEC Crisis of 1965–66. By mid-1965 the European Community was entering a critical period in which all its basic postulates were once more being questioned. As a noted student of European integration was later to conclude, this was "the most serious crisis" in the Community's history.[28] The most devastating aspect was France's rejection of "supranationalism," "integration," and "atlanticism" — the three basic goals of Italian foreign policy since 1949, which had been consistently advocated by most political parties. Yet even now the EEC did not become a very prominent issue in Italian politics. While important decisions were being made at the EEC level, the primary focus of the parties' activity outside of purely domestic matters was the Vietnamese conflict and the question of the recognition of Communist China. Even after de Gaulle's assertion that Italy's position on the Agricultural Fund had been the major reason for the June 30th breakdown in negotiations at Brussels, the parties did not change their focus of interest.[29] As indicated in greater detail on pages 40–45, Italy's agricultural policy (domestically and at the EEC level) was a contradictory mixture of economic nationalism and political irresponsibility that clearly militated against regional integration. Yet none of the party elites showed any interest in this.

In commenting on the tensions within the EEC, the party press seemed unconcerned about the future of the regional process; it concentrated primarily on the possible negative impact that the crisis might have on European-American relations or on specific economic interests that could be harmed by the EEC. Meetings of the leadership of various parties did not produce a substantive analysis of the crisis and of Italy's role (in contrast to the extensive and detailed attention given to NATO issues at the same meetings).[30] The government spokesmen merely stated that Italy would press for a resolution of the EEC crisis without compromising the country's basic goals regarding European unity. But such assertions confirmed the superficiality of the government's response, for the EEC crisis was in part due to Italy's unwillingness to reconsider its approach to the regional process. In fact, the 1965–66 crisis as well as the Italian reaction to the French veto of 1963 and the Fouchet Plan are representative of a general pattern of response by the political parties to EEC-related developments.

The total record of parliamentary activity in the 1958–1970 period confirms this pattern.[31] There was very little interest in initiating measures relating to general developments in the EEC, and no concern for European integration itself. Virtually all parliamentary activity connected with the EEC dealt with specific economic interests that had been negatively affected by the process of regional integration; it was, moreover, aimed at seeking protection for those interests from a purely nationalistic viewpoint. By contrast, during the same twelve-year period, all parties followed international developments and NATO-related issues in particular with considerable interest and attempted to influence the government's response to those events. An analysis of various reactions to the MLF project will highlight these conclusions.

The first meeting of the Senate Foreign Affairs Committee after the 1963 French veto was called to receive and discuss a government report on the EEC situation; yet the parties' primary attention was directed to the MLF project.[32] The responses to the MLF and to the EEC seemed to be inversely proportional to political reality. There was no pressure, domestic or international, for a decision on the MLF project; in addition, the international consequences of Italy's position on the MLF could only be minimal. On the other hand, the crisis which was developing within the European Community demanded immediate and potentially critical decisions for Italy; its responses could have a significant impact on future developments within the Community.

The outstanding importance of the MLF for all parties could not be explained by its significance as a foreign policy issue involving strategic commitments for the country. In fact, throughout this period, the government continued to assert that the MLF project had been accepted in principle only, and that no final commitment would be made without prior parliamentary authorization. Essentially, the overriding concern with the MLF derived from the fact that it was a NATO-related issue. As had been the case with the NATO commitment in 1949 and later, the MLF was transformed into a symbol around which various political groups waged their factional and inter-party battles in support of, or in opposition to, a Center-Left coalition government. This case, in fact, is an excellent illustration of the general process of internalization of NATO issues, and to a lesser extent of Italy's foreign policy as a whole. And this process in turn explains why NATO and the EEC were regarded as vastly different in importance by the Italian political elites.

DYNAMICS OF INTERNALIZATION

Recent writings on comparative and international politics have called attention to the impact of external events on the internal behavior of nations, whereby external actors "participate directly and authoritatively, through actions taken jointly with the society's members, in either the allocation of its values or the mobilization of support on behalf of its goals." [33] This process, however, can be sufficiently transformed so that external actors do not directly affect and penetrate domestic politics. External issues can be utilized at the national level for their symbolic significance apart from their actual substantive importance, thus resulting in the "internalization" of international developments. This process aptly describes Italy's relationship with the Atlantic Alliance and, to some extent, with the European Economic Community as well.

Since the early 1950s, the pervasive struggle within and among parties concerning the prospect of a Center-Left coalition government has centered on two interrelated issues: the Socialist party's relationship with the Communists, and its negative attitude towards NATO. All the various groups opposed to the formation of a Center-Left coalition have justified their objections on these two grounds. By the early 1960s, as the links between the PSI and the PCI were definitely severed, efforts to prevent the establishment of a Center-Left government focused on NATO as the critical factor. Hence the significance of the MLF project. Conservative groups could point to Socialist reservations about the MLF as confirmation of their contention that a Center-Left regime would result in a weakening of Italy's NATO commitment. On the other hand, the extreme Left could point to the PSI's partial acquiescence to the MLF as an indication of the party's surrender to the Western military block, and thus hope to cause a rift within the Socialist ranks that would undermine the Center-Left efforts. Caught between the pressure of its Center group to support the MLF and the pressure of its left-wing faction to reject it, the PSI took an ambiguous stand that was to be utilized by the opponents of the Center-Left coalition.[34]

Thus, during the first two precarious years of the Center-Left government in 1963–65, the MLF issue remained a critical factor that often stalemated the coalition. Yet there was no discernible reason for the MLF to become such a controversial issue within the Italian political arena other than the fact that it was a significant international symbol that could be internalized. It was more effective for conservative groups to attempt to undermine the Center-Left coalition in the name of Atlantic orthodoxy than in the name of their opposition to the coalition's social policies: a majority of the electorate and of factions within the DC could respond to the NATO symbolism, but only a small minority was opposed to the socio-economic orientation of the Center-Left coalition.

EEC issues have also been utilized for domestic political purposes; but because their symbolic significance was more limited, the internalization process was to be less intense, even if equally pervasive. For instance, right-wing parties and conservative factions within the DC have frequently argued that because of the EEC commitment Italy should not embark on socialist-oriented economic policies, such policies being contrary to the aims of the Treaty of Rome.

On the other hand, leftist groups have insisted that effective support for European integration could only be provided by a Center-Left government. In their efforts to undermine the Center-Left government, conservative groups have argued that the Socialist party's presence in the coalition government was responsible for Italy's negative and ambiguous role within the European Community and thus contributed to the EEC crises. These groups have insisted that in order to promote European unity, Italy should install a government without the Socialist party. Although the European Community ostensibly received great attention within the DC, a close analysis of party meetings and policy discussions shows no concern for the integration process. It was given little attention even during periods of serious Community crises when the party elites could have played an important role by influencing the government's response.[35] To a large extent, then, the EEC was merely used as an instrument in the internal party struggle.

The internalization of foreign policy issues is, of course, related to the nature of the political system. In an unstable system with stalemating tendencies, frequent governmental crises, and constant political maneuvering within and among parties, exploitation of foreign policy for internal purposes is almost inevitable. Thus, during the period of virtually every EEC crisis, government coalition maneuvers were under way in Italy; and this, of course, hampered the ability of parties to focus on the regional process. Because NATO is of great symbolic significance for these domestic developments, attention to Alliance issues actually increased during periods of domestic political crisis. The EEC, on the other hand, is of only limited importance for the domestic battle, and thus concern for regional developments has been negatively affected by the continual political crisis in Italy. In both cases, however, the significance of regional and Alliance developments was determined by their *domestic* importance — the extent to which they could be internalized — rather than by their substance or the nature of NATO and the EEC.

In the case of NATO, the internalization process could be of little consequence for the Alliance itself: whether or not Italy was genuinely making a positive contribution to NATO, the potential impact of her behavior would be quite minimal. In the case of the EEC, on the other hand, the internalization process was to be critical in two ways. It helped make the Italian parties impervious to EEC pressures for a redirection of narrow domestic concerns to the wider scope of the European Community. And it contributed to the Italian government's inability to formulate and implement a coherent European policy and to play a positive role at the Community level. A policy aimed at integration naturally requires concern for regional developments and a shift in expectations and attitudes towards a new focus; the internalization process results in the exploitation of regional developments for domestic purposes, with no consideration for its impact on integration. Basically, the low priority assigned to EEC issues and their partial internalization also demonstrate the parties' superficial commitment to regional integration and their perception of the EEC as a mere economic entity with limited importance for domestic politics. NATO developments, however, have always been given much greater attention because the Atlantic Alliance has been perceived as a significant component of the domestic political struggle.

NATO AS A POLITICAL CONTEXT

From the beginning, apart from domestic political considerations, Italy's attitude towards NATO has been determined not so much by a concern for security as by its search for a role in world politics. Italy's interest in questions of military strategy has been minimal; its major effort has been to gain recognition as an important member of the Alliance. For this reason, every Italian government since 1949 has opposed all attempts to create a directorate within NATO because it would have meant a special role for the great powers and Italy's exclusion from that rank. Italy's frequent efforts at playing a mediatory role within the Atlantic context also are an expression of its search for an active international presence. Thus, despite its strong assertions of commitment to the Atlantic Alliance, in actual behavior Italy has not been a solid supporter of NATO as a *military* organization. Rather it has tended to remain uninvolved in virtually every crisis affecting the Alliance's military posture.

It is therefore not surprising that since 1950 Italy's allocations for defense in relation to GNP have been the lowest among the NATO countries.[36] During the mid-1960s, Italy objected to an increase in national military contributions as demanded by NATO strategic plans, justifying its stand by budgetary considerations. Yet, during the same period Italy was actively pursuing a greater role in the Mediterranean area independently of NATO, a goal which involved a potential increase in armaments. Parliamentary debates on defense budgets indicate that there is no relationship between the strategic objectives established by NATO's military command and the resources actually allocated to defense in Italy. The defense budget, in fact, is primarily determined by domestic political needs and bargaining; little or no attention is given to the military contributions expected of Italy within NATO. Despite its willingness to accept American leadership politically and strategically, in practice Italy has been most reluctant to translate its acquiescence into cooperation.[37]

Even Italy's acceptance of missile bases in the late 1950s, despite the widespread opposition within the country, only appeared to be a sign of military support for NATO. In accepting missile bases in the era of Sputnik and in the face of strong Soviet objections, Italy might be viewed as willing to accept risks in order to contribute to the strategic needs of NATO. As in the case of the MLF plan, however, the major reason behind Italy's decision was purely political: Italian leaders expected to increase the country's status within the Atlantic Alliance as a result of missile installations.[38] In other words, even purely strategic decisions were approached in terms of prestige rather than security considerations.

Several historical and social factors account for the tendency to respond to NATO in political terms. During the 1949 debates on the Atlantic Treaty, a significant portion of the Italian political elite — a wide group cutting across many parties — had strong objections to *any* military alliance. This anti-militarist tendency did not disappear after 1949. It was merely obfuscated by the frequent assertions of unquestioning commitment to the Alliance that were uttered by the government parties and leaders for two decades. Policy declarations notwithstanding, a widespread — albeit latent — pacifism permeates the Italian political scene — the public at large, the political parties, and the government itself.

A significant section of the public assigns little importance to NATO as a military alliance. A poll conducted in 1958, when the cold war had by no means abated, showed that only fifty percent of the respondents favored Italy's continued membership in the Alliance.[39] Among the political parties, too, there always has been substantial opposition to the military aspect of NATO. In effect, the Liberal party, the right-wing DC, the right-wing Social Democrats, and the neo-Fascists (which together account for a quarter of the electorate) are the only political forces that have consistently shown a firm commitment, in official declarations and in actual behavior, to NATO as a military alliance. The Communist party and the PSIUP (the left-wing socialist party organized in 1964), which between them account for a solid third of the electorate, are definitely anti-NATO. The Communists have actually modified their pro-Soviet stand to a more neutralist posture which calls for the elimination of both the Western and the Eastern bloc; but this is far from accepting NATO itself. The Socialist party still retains a strong neutralist-pacifist orientation that has not been affected by the party's official acceptance of the rhetoric of the government and the Christian Democrats regarding the Atlantic Alliance.[40]

The Christian Democratic party itself contains groups that have tended to see NATO as at best a temporary necessity. In addition, the DC is strongly influenced by an amorphous, but potentially powerful, Catholic internationalism which again makes the commitment somewhat precarious and temporary.[41] At times the very vehemence of the DC leaders' affirmations of "fidelity" to NATO was perhaps intended to compensate for the underlying anti-Alliance feelings within the party. The domestic and international situation has not permitted an explicit expression of these underlying attitudes; but they have remained strong, and by the late 1960s some DC factions were openly beginning to formulate alternative conceptions of international politics as well as denouncing NATO as an instrument of conservative entrenchment. More subtly, in recent years, these groups within the DC have been pushing the party and the government in the direction of a policy of working towards the dissolution of both NATO and the Eastern bloc.

Occasionally, Christian Democratic government leaders have pursued this tendency in the form of revisionism within the Atlantic Alliance. In the 1950s, for instance, President Giovanni Gronchi tried to convert NATO into an instrument of détente. In a speech to the United States Congress, in February 1956, Gronchi affirmed that NATO was no longer adequate and that it should be transformed from a military alliance into a wider community aimed at international cooperation. Amintore Fanfani, as prime minister or foreign minister in various governments, has promoted policies which have often shown signs of neutralism going beyond the confines of the NATO commitment.[42]

An important reason for this situation is to be found in the link between NATO and domestic politics. In 1958, for instance, the same factions within the DC that were demanding a revisionist stand towards the Alliance were also pressing for a "dialogue" with the Italian Communist party. The Fanfani cabinet fell in 1959 when conservative groups in the DC withdrew their support, claiming that the government's "revisionist" foreign policy would weaken the Atlantic Alliance and Italy's commitment to it. Since the Fanfani government was not about to destroy the Alliance, it was quite clear that NATO was being used as a pretext; the actual objection was to the possibility of an entente between the Center parties and the Socialists that Fanfani was then promoting with some success. In effect, for two decades, the left-wing groups that were opposed to NATO also sought to create a different domestic political system. On the other hand, the Center and Right regarded the Atlantic link as a necessary complement for the identity and stability of the system itself. During this period, however, the pressure of powerful opposition from the Left, the instability of the political system, and the influence of socio-economic factors all combined to rule out the introduction of new perspectives into the domestic debate as well as reconsideration of the related symbolic importance of the NATO link.

In such a context the prospect for change and political realignments came to be seen as closely dependent on the evolution of the international situation and Italy's foreign policy. Hence the demands by the leftist parties for a change in the country's relationship with NATO as an indispensable precondition for the opposition's collaboration in the political system.[43] With the transformation of the cold war the demands of the Left regarding NATO also became less rigid. The Socialist party moved from a neutralist stand (and total rejection of NATO) in 1949 to a limited acceptance of the Alliance in the 1950s; and eventually to complete acquiescence by 1962 in conjunction with the party's entry into the government coalition. The Communist party changed from a pro-Soviet to a neutralist stand in the late 1960s in connection with its overtures towards the DC and the PSI for a domestic entente of the three parties.

A similar development occurred within the DC itself. As indicated earlier, even in 1949 left-wing groups within the DC were opposed to Italy's entry into NATO because they feared it would remove all chances of collaboration between the center and the leftist parties. For two decades the conflict within the DC continued unabated, with NATO as the constant point of reference. While the dominant Center-Right groups insisted on Atlantic orthodoxy as a rationale for resisting any collaboration between the DC and the leftist parties, the minority Center-Left groups pressed for a flexible attitude towards NATO as a way of promoting that collaboration.[44]

Since the DC perceived NATO as largely defining the orientation of the Italian political system, the continuous battle within the party since 1953 regarding the possibility of a Center-Left government was directly affected by the Atlantic commitment. The MLF case was an illustration of this pattern: the MLF assumed prominence within Italy not because of its obvious connection with issues of strategy and national security but because of its potential impact on the Center-Left coalition government. The DC reactions to the 1968 Soviet invasion of Czechoslovakia provide a more recent example. Center-Right groups within the DC perceived the Czech crisis as a serious threat to détente and security, and thus wished to see NATO strengthened as a military organization. On the other hand, the left-wing groups within the party saw the crisis as an indication of the cold war's demise and demanded further détente moves from NATO.

In effect, however, all factions within the DC were mainly concerned with the domestic implications of the Czech crisis.[45] For one faction, a rigid pro-NATO stand was aimed at strengthening its uncompromising attitude towards the role of the Communist party within the Italian political system. For the opposing faction, further détente and a related transformation of the Alliance were seen as indispensable to achieve a coalition between the DC and the Left. As Table 1 shows, there is a high correlation between views on domestic politics and certain positions regarding the Atlantic Alliance. As late as 1969, when the Center-Left coalition was embroiled in a serious crisis triggered by overtures of collaboration by the Communists, the battle was still carried on in terms of NATO as much as those of purely domestic concerns. By becoming a preponderant context for domestic politics, the Atlantic relationship has also negatively affected Italy's response to European integration.

Table 1

CORRELATION BETWEEN DOMESTIC AND FOREIGN POLICY

This chart is derived from various positions expressed by Christian Democratic faction leaders at the DC party executive's meeting of November 1968. Though many issues and controversies were involved, it was quite clear from all the documents and speeches that essentially the battle centered on *two* critical issues: (a) the relationship between Italy and NATO; (b) the relationship between the DC, the government coalition, and the Communist party.

DC FACTIONS	STAND ON DOMESTIC POLITICS	STAND ON FOREIGN POLICY
Left-wing (Base, Forze Nuove, Fanfaniani)	— open attitude towards the PCI to test that party's willingness to participate in the political system; — in favor of greater planning and more radical policies	— very critical of passive acceptance of NATO position; — demand gradual elimination of Eastern and Western bloc as well as of spheres of influence; détente efforts; China's admission to the UN
Center (Morotei, Dorotei)	— want continuation of the moderate Center-Left government of 1963-68; — no dialogue with the PCI	— absolute "fidelity" to NATO, which is seen as "scelta di civiltà" and essential to stability
Right (Tavianei, Centristi, Primavera)	— must retain rigid separation between the government coalition and PCI; — government must defend and aid a free market economy and resist any socialist pressures for planning	— the basic hard-line NATO policies of the past must remain unchanged; — vigilance rather than openness towards the East; — NATO and Atlantic solidarity must be reinforced

(The Right and Center-Right regarded NATO not only as indispensable but also as demanding a type of political system in Italy that would completely preclude any possible accommodation with the extreme Left.)

3. Italy's Behavior Towards the European Community

Italy has participated in every postwar effort aimed at promoting European unity. Even in cases such as the Coal and Steel Community, which was strongly opposed by powerful industrial groups, the Italian government firmly supported integrative moves. The process of integration, however, involves much more than the original governmental decision to support the creation of institutions such as the EEC; at the level of inter-governmental cooperation the regional process soon reaches a plateau. A continuing commitment is needed for genuine integration to occur, a commitment involving the political will of government and parties to stimulate integrative developments both domestically and at the regional level.

For this reason, a country's commitment and contribution to integration cannot be appraised simply on the basis of its declared policy or its acts of official support for regional organizations. The critical test will be the country's willingness to relinquish a purely national position and to accept the domestic consequences of the regional process. At the economic level, a country's willingness to accept the elimination of tariffs in accordance with the regional scheme would not be a sufficient indicator; the country's behavior regarding the domestic enforcement of those obligations provides the critical test — for instance, does the government seek to elude the removal of tariffs through hidden tax incentives? Politically, a country's commitment to supranationality implies a willingness to accept the authority and rules of the regional organization, even if the result may be a curtailment of domestic political interests.

From this perspective, Italy has not been a strong supporter of European political and economic integration. Domestically, the Italian government has often carried out policies in direct contradiction to its avowed commitment to regional unification; it has violated both the spirit and the letter of the Treaty of Rome, opting for positions that clearly damaged the integration process. The various political parties have either been uninterested and unresponsive or have supported anti-integrative policies as often as pro-integration moves. There has been no significant indication, at the party level, of an acceptance of regional unification as something other than a remote foreign policy matter.

INTEGRATIVE BEHAVIOR AT THE DOMESTIC LEVEL

The Government. In their actual behavior, various Italian governments since 1948 have frequently acted counter to their declared policy of support for economic and political unity in Europe. For instance, for over a decade Italy advocated direct elections of representatives to the European Parliament. But nothing was ever done by the Italian government to realize this objective despite the introduction of specific bills in Parliament requesting its implementation in Italy even if no agreement could be reached at the Community level.[46] Even more revealing is the fact that, for ten years, successive governments failed to fill vacancies in the Italian delegation to the European Parliament, in complete disregard of their own protestations and of provisions of the Treaty of Rome requiring the reappointment of members of the European Parliament after each national election. As a result, of thirty-six seats assigned to Italy, only seven were filled during the 1960s. Thus in a period when the most delicate phase of the EEC was to unfold, Italy was virtually unrepresented at the European assembly.

Why this incongruity between policy declarations and actual behavior? Vacancies to the European Parliament could not be filled because the government coalition could not agree on a common policy towards the Communist party; the entire issue was shelved in order to avoid a confrontation that might destroy the precarious Center-Left government. Yet the opposition of the Center parties to seating Italian Communist delegates in the European Parliament reveals the shallowness of their commitment to European integration: their objection to including the PCI in the Italian delegation was based on the claim that the party was opposed to European unification, although by the early 1960s it had generally accepted the EEC. This explanation, of course, contradicted the government's efforts within the EEC to have representatives to the European Parliament elected directly, which would assure the presence of Communist members in the Italian delegation since the PCI easily controls one fourth of the electorate.[47]

Although strong advocates of economic integration, Italian governments have frequently disregarded EEC statutes and policies. Italy has often failed to respond to EEC demands and regulations, and it has also flagrantly damaged the integrative process by both action and inaction. Symptomatic of this behavior is the large number of cases brought against Italy in the European Court of Justice, which was established to settle disputes within the EEC. Another illustration can be found in Italy's reactions to the tax coordination efforts within the EEC. Tax coordination represents a very important step towards the creation of a

[29]

genuine common market and eventually an economic union. In 1967 the EEC countries agreed to establish by January 1970 a uniform Value Added Tax (VAT) system. The Italian business community clearly expressed its support. There were no seemingly insurmountable barriers to its implementation, and the Italian government fully agreed with the 1967 EEC decision. Yet two years after the original unanimous decision at the EEC Council of Ministers no legislative steps had been taken in Italy to reform its revenue system by incorporating VAT in it. Meanwhile, by 1969, all other EEC countries (with the partial exception of Belgium) were implementing the VAT system despite some negative effects on their own economies. In Holland, for instance, although the adoption of VAT contributed to an inflationary trend, the government proceeded to implement the EEC agreement on schedule. In May 1969, Italy announced that it could not adopt the new taxation system on time and that it would need at least two more years beyond the January 1970 deadline.

Belgium had also asked for a postponement, but its handling of the situation was marked by a different attitude towards the EEC. The Belgian government sent a memorandum to the EEC Commission explaining the economic problems that had made the request for an extension necessary and formally asked the EEC Council of Ministers for permission to postpone implementation. The Belgian government thus demonstrated its acceptance of the EEC process: it requested a decision by the European Community before submitting legislation to the national parliament that would alter the original EEC agreement on VAT. By contrast, the Italian government merely notified the European Commission of its inability to adopt the VAT system and of its decision to delay implementation.[48] This case fits into the pattern of Italian responses to the European Community. Italian leaders willingly support every EEC step towards regional unification; yet, when it comes to actual realization of EEC-level decisions, there is a tendency to delay and to seek modifications to accommodate purely domestic needs and interests. Above all, the necessary leadership and political will to move the country in the direction of integration seems to be lacking. A major reason is the nature of the political system: its dynamics are such that policy declarations, and even specific commitments to the EEC, cannot be easily translated into legislation. Frequently, stalemate and inaction are the only possible options for precarious coalition governments constantly on the verge of collapse. The mere fact that a Community decision may be widely supported by the major economic forces in the country is no assurance of its implementation.

Beyond those instances in which Italy's failure to carry out its EEC obligations stemmed from certain features of its political system, the government on many occasions also deliberately opposed EEC principles and policies. Its response to the EEC's Court of Justice is one example of unwillingness to accept the Community process. In several cases involving complaints of Italian infractions of EEC regulations the government claimed that the European Court of Justice lacked jurisdiction. In addition, the Italian government has also rejected the principle of supranationality — the same principle that, in policy declarations, Italy has been supporting vehemently since the late 1940s as indispensable for regional unification.[49] The superficiality of the country's commitment to the European Community can also be seen in the government's handling of the 1963-64 economic crisis in Italy. Instead of following the recommendations of the EEC Commission, the Italian government turned directly to the United States for a loan to redress Italy's balance of payments difficulties. This action was in clear disregard of the EEC, at a time when the Commission was seeking to promote a common EEC stand vis-à-vis the "Kennedy Round" negotiations. A similar attitude can also be noted in Italy's planning process. The Five Year Plan for 1965-69, for instance, involved many years of bargaining among various pressure groups, parties, and government leaders; yet, throughout that process, no effort was made to relate the plan to the European Community directly or indirectly, nor did the final formulation of the plan contain any reference to the EEC.[50]

Another consistent pattern of behavior in Italy's response to the EEC is an uncompromising defense of national interests. There is nothing unusual about a country seeking to promote its interests: the process of regional unification normally combines the espousal of domestic interests with a willingness to sacrifice in some areas in order to facilitate integration. The Italian record, however, shows an unvarying tendency to resist any regional developments not in accord with explicit national gains. Much attention has been given to the French opposition to the European Atomic Energy Community (Euratom), such as the French request of December 1968 aimed at reducing the scope and role of the organization. But a year before, in December 1967, Italy had already requested a similar reduction in Euratom programs. In the rhetoric of its demands, Italy stressed its great commitment to integration: Euratom had allegedly failed to develop a common and supranational policy. In reality, the Italian government was dissatisfied with Euratom because the country had not derived sufficient benefits from Euratom's projects. For this reason Italy wanted to reduce the amount of its financial contributions and limit the scope of Euratom's activities, which in effect meant a limitation of the supranational aspects of the

[31]

organization. When France made similar demands in December 1968, Italian leaders immediately attributed Euratom's problems to the French; the Italian government itself, however, had already contributed to reducing Euratom's integrative potential.[51]

In essence, the government has worked towards integration (as distinguished from officially paying lip service to it) only if and when the European Community seemed likely to benefit Italy economically or politically. Euratom did not appear to be sufficiently advantageous from either perspective. Another example is Italy's 1966 "Technological Marshall Plan," a proposal aimed at narrowing the technological gap between Europe and the United States.[52] Instead of focusing on European institutions, the plan would actually have increased American participation in Europe — a prospect that was objectionable to France and inconsistent with the process of regional integration. But the Italian government, preeminently concerned with domestic needs and interests, failed to realize that the reversal of priorities implied in the plan would negatively affect Italy's role within the European Community. This pattern of response has not changed in recent years. For instance, in May 1974 Italy suddenly imposed import restrictions in order to deal with a growing financial crisis partly related to its international trade balance. Yet despite the obvious negative effect of import restrictions on the Common Market, Italy's decision was made and announced unilaterally — without even consulting its EEC partners.

A commitment to integration also implies a willingness by the various governments to contribute to the regional bureaucracy not only by making their own civil servants available, but by providing incentives for them to join the European administration while guaranteeing seniority within the national civil service. In addition, it implies a willingness to adapt the national administrations to the needs and demands of the regional organization. These are two particularly critical requirements because, to carry out its tasks, the EEC is still dependent on the administrative structures of the member countries.[53] Yet the Italian record stands out for its inadequacies in both respects.

At the national level, the chronic inefficiency and unresponsiveness of the Italian bureaucracy has shown no significant signs of change. Despite recurrent pressure from the EEC and from domestic groups demanding greater efficiency and speedier implementation of EEC regulations, the government has not generated the political will to bring about the needed reforms in the bureaucracy. At the EEC administrative level, Italy has been notable for its consistent record of indifference and inactivity. It has lagged behind other countries in moving its administrators into the EEC bureaucracy and in the caliber of its representation at EEC inter-governmental meetings. Since 1958, with few exceptions, Italy has not sent its best administrators to Brussels. Positions reserved for Italy within the EEC Commission have often remained unfilled for several months. There is no scarcity of able European-minded Italians, but in the absence of government incentives it is to the disadvantage of an Italian civil servant to serve in Brussels.[54]

The Italian bureaucracy has tended to perceive European Community matters as marginal and remote. EEC-related initiatives have been largely relegated to the Ministry of Foreign Affairs, as if they were matters of foreign policy exclusively. The various technical ministries have successfully resisted the pressures for change resulting from the regional process and have continued to give rigid priority to local interests. This situation, combined with the dearth of first-rate Italian representatives in Community institutions, has led to a marked lack of cooperation between the national administration and the EEC agencies. While the Ministry of Foreign Affairs has been quite competent and active, it lacks the technical expertise and the political influence of the specialized ministries and has thus only in part succeeded in compensating for their unwillingness and inability to deal with EEC-related developments in a constructive and supportive manner.[55]

This failure at the administrative level cannot be merely ascribed to bureaucratic obstructionism; it derives from the absence of a political will at the governmental and party level to take a firm stand in promoting the necessary responses and adjustments required by the European Community. It is the political system — which makes it virtually impossible for strong leadership to emerge and to be exercised effectively — that largely accounts for this situation. The precariousness of the system and its frequent crises have also affected the government's ability to provide adequate representation at the various EEC ministerial meetings. For instance, a typical sample of attendance at EEC meetings in the 1964–66 period shows that more than 30 percent of the time undersecretaries represented the appropriate minister. In terms of concrete results, of course, an undersecretary usually is technically more competent than a minister; but the important issue is the subtle difference in political influence, particularly during a period as politically critical for the EEC as the years 1964–66.

It has been assumed in the neo-functionalist theory of regionalism — the predominant theory since the 1950s — that so long as major parties, leaders, and interest groups were committed to integration, the process would continue without difficulty.[56] This kind of commitment does exist in Italy; yet the country's behavior has frequently been opposed to integration and thus to its own commitments. It may be concluded that although the component parts of a political system may be fully committed to regional unification, their positive role may be effectively undermined by the dynamics of the system itself. The process of integration involves a shifting of expectations and orientations from a national focus to a wider regional context. Because of the determining role played by the parties, the impact of the integrative process ought to be particularly apparent there.

The Political Parties. As previously noted, the Christian Democratic elites have approached European unification as merely an aspect of the Atlantic link and have thus strongly objected to any scheme for further integration that might lead to greater autonomy for Europe. The DC also tends to see European integration as another weapon in its fight against communism.[57] This has contributed to the party's failure to realize that the EEC requires a new kind of political behavior. Typical DC assertions merely reiterate vague assurances of "fidelity" to the EEC, while indicating no real grasp of the issues involved and of the actual policies necessary to achieve concrete results. The party, for instance, supported Britain's entry into the EEC, even though Britain was opposed to the supranational aspects of the Community. This did not prevent the DC from pressing for a supranational Europe moving towards a political union, without apparently noticing the incongruity of the two goals.

The superficial and limited attention bestowed on the EEC by Christian-Democratic elites also stems from the dynamics of the Italian political system and the resulting internecine battles within each party. At virtually every DC leadership meeting, for instance, the profusion of domestic problems tends to generate intra-party disputes so that little interest or energy is left for Community issues which cannot be utilized in the internal struggle.[58]

Despite its reservations regarding the EEC in 1957, by 1960–61 the Socialist party was fully supporting the goal of European integration. Following its entry into the coalition government in 1962–63, the PSI assumed many of the positions of the Christian Democratic party on virtually every major aspect of the European Community: commitment to political and economic integration, demand for a stronger European Parliament, opposition to de Gaulle's European vision, and support for Britain's admission to the EEC. This convergence of views notwithstanding, the domestic political struggle has at times resulted in direct conflict between the Socialists and the DC concerning European issues. For example, the Socialists' insistence on including Communist party representatives in the Italian delegation to the European Parliament produced a stalemate that for a decade prevented new appointments from being made. Although the Socialists justified their position with references to the Treaty of Rome, in effect their rigid position derived primarily from their interest in promoting the PCI as an acceptable party domestically.[59] Hence, a purely internal dispute was responsible for the anomaly of Italy's virtual non-representation in the European Parliament during the 1960s.

The Socialists have tended to utilize the EEC not only in support of a planning policy in Italy but also in building up the European Community as an alternative to the country's inflexible Atlantic orientation. Because of the diverging position of the DC on both issues, however, the EEC became a point of dispute within the Center-Left coalition government and accordingly failed to generate supportive responses at the party and governmental levels. The PSI pressed for the admission of Britain and the Scandinavian countries because it expected their membership to increase the size and influence of socialist groups within the expanded Community. Convinced that genuine economic integration and planning on a European scale are essential to promote the interests of the working class, the party insisted on those countries' admission as a way of maximizing its influence. But in the pursuit of these goals it failed to realize that a certain degree of political integration may be necessary to produce a genuine economic union capable of instituting regional planning. In effect, consumed by internecine battles over the party's role within the coalition government and its relations with the PCI, the Socialists were forced to approach the EEC as an ancillary instrument in their domestic efforts.[60] Hence their inability to devote adequate attention to the EEC as a regional process.

Although the Communist party's position regarding the EEC has undergone a significant change since 1957, its impact on Italy's integrative behavior domestically and at the EEC level has remained basically negative. By 1960 the PCI was no longer advocating the abolition of the EEC, and by 1962 it was acknowledging the Community's generally beneficial effects on the Italian economy.[61] After 1963, the party also began to campaign for full representation in EEC organizations to promote its role as defender of working-class interests. At the same time, the party pressed for a type of regional unification that in effect was directly opposed to the vision and aims implicit in the Treaty of Rome. It vehemently opposed the supranational aspects of the EEC, proposing as an alternative an "integrative" structure open to both Eastern and Western Europe and to the underdeveloped countries as well. Regarding this alternative as indispensable for ridding the EEC of "reactionary" and "monopolistic" domination, the Communists consistently campaigned for the retention of complete national control of the regional process — specifically in the hands of national parliaments — in order to prevent "the exploitation of the EEC by international capitalist groups." [62]

On particular EEC-related domestic issues the PCI has also provided a negative stimulus. The party has, for instance, presented a reasonable analysis of Italy's agricultural problems, stressing the need for structural reforms as an alternative to the customary protectionist policy of subsidies and price control; but this effort merely aimed at buttressing the party's campaign against the supranational aspects of the EEC rather than at bringing about appropriate policy changes at the national and the regional level. Because EEC policies caused some real economic hardships no definite causal link can be established between the PCI's position and the general trend of anti-Community feeling in many sectors of Italian agriculture by the late 1960s. However, the overall record of parliamentary activity in the 1960s shows that Communist interventions on EEC matters were aimed at highlighting specific economic problems that could be attributed to Italy's membership in the EEC.[63] The PCI has thus contributed to the tendency of other parties to devote virtually all their attention to a parochial defense of economic interests, with little regard for the wider scope of European integration.

The parties, then, have played a minimal role as promoters of the EEC, and in many instances have actually impeded its development. Even during periods of severe crisis in the Community, as has been shown, the parties' concern for the regional process was extremely limited. They displayed little inclination to generate the domestic responses that are necessary for integration to take place. Nor did they exhibit any substantial initiative in support of measures and actions that might promote political and economic unification in Europe. That is, the parties' commitment to integration did not produce a political will to implement it.[64] Expectations and attitudes were not redirected away from a purely national focus. Whenever national economic interests were involved, the parties have indeed looked upon the EEC as a significant force; but they have strenuously resisted going beyond a mere defense of those interests from a nationalistic perspective. There has been little awareness of the likelihood that the European process would not develop beyond a mere common market unless the parties themselves were willing to promote and support integrative responses at the domestic level. Various organizations of national parties at the EEC level can, at best, produce a *Europe des États* (that is, a confederation of states still retaining their political autonomy). It is at the national level that a revolution in attitudes and behavior must occur if integration is to take place, and it is at this level that the least change has occurred.

The intense and continuous political battle within Italy greatly affects the parties' ability to respond to the regional process. The few leaders, mostly left-wing Socialists and left-wing Christian Democrats, who have pointed to the incongruities in Italy's position regarding European unification and the Atlantic relationship have been submerged by the rhetoric of anti-communism and the related claim that firm NATO links are of vital importance. As a result, the substance of EEC developments and its basic purpose — matters that were particularly critical in the 1960s — were completely ignored. For instance, the government has tended to request decree powers at the beginning of each phase of implementation of the Treaty of Rome in order to avoid parliamentary debates on EEC negotiations, which invariably provoked Communist polemics. While justifiable from the standpoint of efficiency, this approach has contributed to preventing parties and public from exerting influence on EEC developments. Uninvolved in the process of regional integration, the parties have instead championed the claims of specific economic interests in opposition to the government's advocacy of a supranational orientation.

Interest Groups and the General Public. In a reappraisal of the European Community published in 1968, Ernst Haas concluded that although public opinion had generally been in favor of European unity throughout the previous two decades, it still remained "impressionistic, weakly structured, and lacking in patterns of demands and expectations — except among young people."[65] Similarly, writing in 1971, Joseph Nye affirmed that "despite popular expressions favorable to regional organization, opinion in Europe and elsewhere has tended to provide only a permissive consensus rather than a clear direction."[66]

Recent studies by other European and American scholars confirm these conclusions.[67] They are fully applicable to the Italian case. Despite a vague interest in European unification, expressed by most newspapers, there is no indication of a substantive commitment to genuine political and economic integration. There is no significant pressure from the public for integration beyond the existing customs union. The vague commitment to European unity that most parties and elites display seems to satisfy the general public; there is no widespread demand for greater efforts by the parties and government in the direction of further integration. Organized groups, such as the Italian section of the European Federalist Movement, which advocate initiatives by Italy in promoting regional unification, have no mass base; they are restricted to very small intellectual circles, and their influence has actually dwindled since the early 1950s.[68]

The extent of a party's commitment to European unity seems to be of little relevance to the electorate. EEC issues are not an important aspect of electoral programs (in contrast to NATO issues, for instance) and have not played a significant role in the outcome of elections. For example, the Communist party's opposition to the Treaty of Rome in 1957 does not seem to have affected its standing in the 1958 national elections. In 1957, the Socialist party abstained on the EEC ratification vote; yet it registered substantial gains in the 1958 elections, despite the fact that other parties — and the Social Democrats in particular — stood forth as firm advocates of European integration.[69]

The Italian public, then, shows a widespread lack of interest in specific EEC developments. A 1962 poll indicated that 64 percent of a general Italian sample was totally uninformed concerning European problems, in contrast to an average 22 percent for similar samples in other EEC countries. Another survey, in 1969, indicated that a majority of respondents in Italy perceived the EEC as an esoteric, only remotely significant organization. It is not surprising that comparative data from the six EEC countries showed that Italy displayed the lowest level of support for European unity.[70] This lack of support may be an additional reason why all parties approach the EEC in extremely vague terms; and in turn this vagueness may contribute to the public's disinterest. As a result, there is no actual or potential public pressure capable of modifying the weak integrative behavior of the political parties.

Although industrial employers' organizations have generally supported the aims of the European Community, their involvement has been limited to the EEC as a "common market;" they have never exerted pressure on the political system to promote integration beyond a customs union.[71] On the contrary, because industrial and business groups in Italy have easy access to the parties and to the government, their demands (usually parochial and limited to specific economic gains) have enhanced the inclination of parties and the government to approach the EEC as a mere intergovernmental agency, an external organization for promoting national economic interests.

Like the political parties, labor unions have established their own agencies at the EEC level. But as in the case of the parties, the existence of such agencies has not resulted in significant changes in the unions' behavior. While vigorously proclaiming acceptance of the regional process, unions have merely made token efforts to redirect their operations towards a European focus; they have not tried to convert their members to a European point of view; nor have they exerted integrative pressures on the parties and the government. Once again, the nature of the political situation in Italy has contributed to such developments. Because of domestic battles related to the role of the Communist party within the political system, the largest labor union confederation (the Communist-influenced CGIL) has been excluded from representation in EEC institutions, such as the Economic and Social Council. This has further weakened the labor unions at the Community level, and it has also meant the exclusion of the large sector of public opinion that is under CGIL influence. Significantly, this discrimination against CGIL has occurred despite the fact that, in contrast with the Communist party, it never opposed the EEC and since 1961 has pressed for direct collaboration with all other unions within the European Community. In fact, CGIL has also openly criticized the Communist party and the World Labor Federation for their objections to the EEC.

Even though they established their own organizations in Brussels, the labor unions have not been able to exert influence on EEC decisions and have thus retained a national focus, pursuing their interests through the parties and the government — even in agricultural matters where one would have expected a merging of regional and national interests.[72] As Jean Monnet and others have recognized, European unity will not be easily achieved without the support of workers' organizations. The record of Italian unions is not encouraging in this respect: both the union leadership and rank and file still regard the European Community as a remote and even inimical entity.

Implications for the Integration Process. In summary, then, Italian political forces have not provided a significant stimulus for greater regional integration. The political system has remained receptive to the impact of pressure groups, even when their demands were in support of short-range economic interests opposed to the European Community. The case of agriculture, especially because it is the area of greatest "integration" within the EEC, provides a good illustration. Agricultural interests in Italy have been noticeably successful in resisting the changes necessary to prepare agriculture for the regional process. By 1968, agricultural groups and most of the political parties as well were firmly resisting the EEC agricultural policy because it had become partially unproductive for the Italian economy. But, as has been noted, regional integration implies a willingness to make sacrifices in some areas so long as the process as a whole appears beneficial; and there is no doubt, within and without Italy, that the country has generally benefited from membership in the EEC.

While one could not expect agricultural interest groups to accept losses voluntarily in the name of integration, parties and the government could be expected to do so on the basis of their commitment to the EEC. Instead, the record shows not only total subservience of the parties and government to special local interests, but also their failure to provide the necessary leadership to bring about the structural changes that were needed in Italian agriculture to make the integrative process beneficial. During the 1957 debates on the Treaty of Rome the major political elites had made a clear commitment to implement radical changes promptly to further the country's adjustment to the EEC common agricultural policy. Little effort in that direction had been made by the late 1960s, and the tendency then was to resist integration itself.

The obvious negativism of France's EEC policy under President de Gaulle provided a convenient alibi for over a decade. Yet, at virtually every level (whether political or narrowly economic) Italian political elites have shown little willingness to accept the necessary domestic consequences of regional unification. The reality of this situation has been obfuscated by a widespread tacit assumption that continuing integration is an automatic, inevitable process. But the emergence of a customs union and the growth of administrative and economic links do not per se produce a supranational structure. Regional integration cannot result from the evolution of existing national practices and orientation; it needs a revolution in the existing national economic and political structures.

In short, integration can only be achieved by an act of political will. Even the establishment of a mere economic union requires a political commitment. This means that the parties (which play the determining role in the national exercise of power, particularly in Italy) must be the essential links for the regional process. As long as the EEC is viewed as an external entity not requiring a basic reorientation and restructuring of national behavior, associations of parties at the EEC level can only produce token results. The lesson of the Soviet-East European common market (COMECON) is revealing. Despite the predominant role of one nation, no genuine integration has been possible because of the resistance of national parties in East European countries.[73] In the EEC case, the neo-functionalist vision of cross-national alliances of parties and interest groups has indeed been nominally realized by the establishment of common organizations in Brussels. But the party structures, their programs and orientations, the locus and focus of their political behavior remain essentially national.

As has been shown, the existence of a strong public commitment to regional integration by the major political elites in a country (as in Italy) is no assurance that they will be able to translate words into action. Besides the various factors already discussed, the stalemating tendencies of the political system also substantially reduce the ability of political elites to respond to the integrative pressures generated by the EEC. Symptomatic of this situation is the inadequacy of Italy's formal policy-making practices for Community matters. These conclusions support the views of those scholars who have been calling attention to political background conditions as playing a much more determining role than had originally been assumed in the early version of the neo-functionalist theory of regional integration.[74]

Italy's formal structure of decision-making and coordination regarding the European Community — centered around the Ministry of Foreign Affairs, which presides over the meetings of the inter-ministerial committee dealing with EEC issues — ought to insure effective and coherent policy. Actually, the structure itself has prevented the formulation of clear objectives and policies because Italy's EEC policy decisions are seldom discussed by the cabinet as a collegial body, or by the appropriate parliamentary committees. Instead, in practice, the directors-general in various ministries have been allowed to determine the Italian response to specific developments related to areas within their jurisdiction without any overall coordination. Since virtually all ministries are effectively dominated by the powerful interest groups they are supposed to regulate, Italy's EEC position has been easily controlled by specific economic interests on an ad hoc basis. For instance, as has already been shown, the Ministry of Agriculture, which has been responsible for Italy's EEC policy on agricultural issues, has mostly been influenced by conservative pressure groups; as a result, during the 1960s, although the most productive response for Italy's economic development would have been a radical restructuring of agriculture (given the country's low agricultural productivity and high costs), these conservative groups instead caused the government to press for greater Community financing while resisting attempts to carry out necessary reforms.[75]

In addition, whenever EEC developments have touched on areas affecting several ministries, almost invariably resulting in conflicting views, the tendency has been for the Ministry of Foreign Affairs to seek a compromise almost as an end in itself. This has often produced positions which were in conflict with the country's general orientation towards the European Community, thus contributing to the government's inability to formulate coherent policies and to play an effective role at the EEC level. Finally, because the government has usually obtained four-year decree-power delegations at the beginning of each phase of the Treaty of Rome, it has been under no legal obligation to consult regularly with Parliament regarding EEC decisions — and in fact it did not do so until 1969. This, in turn, has reinforced Parliament's tendency to either debate broad ideological issues or merely to concentrate on very specific economic interests, in either case failing to become a significant participant in shaping Italy's EEC policy.[76]

The situation does not simply result from institutional-procedural difficulties. The procedures developed to deal with EEC issues reflect the general political conditions in the country: the ambiguities, ideological cleavages, and stalemating tendencies of the system as well as its inability to generate consensus and long-range policy. While the formal structures of policy-making and coordination were largely the products of that system, they also contributed to Italy's failure to translate its general commitment to integration into productive responses domestically and at the Community level.

Integrative Behavior at the EEC Level

Chancellor Konrad Adenauer has written that he regarded European integration as essential for Germany to find a new international role, and to prevent a possible resurgence of nationalism. Similarly, in leading Italy towards a commitment to European unity, Prime Minister Alcide de Gasperi was guided by the conviction that only a structural integration of Italy into Western Europe could resolve the country's chronic problems.[77] It was, in fact, during de Gasperi's premiership that Italy was most active in promoting regional unification along federalist lines. Following the loss by the Christian Democrats of their absolute majority in 1953 and de Gasperi's death a year later, the Italian political system never regained the stability it had enjoyed under his powerful leadership. Since then a sequence of unstable coalition cabinets has been headed by weak leaders frequently chosen for their moderation and mediatory qualities. The lack of strong leadership and of a solid domestic base has contributed to the government's tendency to seek a mediatory role in international relations. This gave the impression of a clear and firm policy which, paradoxically, often resulted from its very absence.

Within the European Community, for instance, the basic pattern of Italy's mediatory role was already set during the 1958 negotiations between the EEC and Britain for the formation of a free trade zone. Italy contributed to the maintenance of unity among the six members of the EEC and successfully forestalled Great Britain's efforts to isolate

France. The positive effect of Italy's mediation in the name of the Treaty of Rome gave the misleading impression that it was pursuing a deliberate policy aimed at promoting regional unification. In fact, the mediatory role resulted from self-interest and from lack of agreement on a coherent policy within the country. This pattern was to continue after 1958, with mediation becoming almost an end in itself because of the government's inability to develop and pursue a substantive policy.

In addition, overshadowing and at times undermining this pattern of behavior has been Italy's perception of NATO as the unquestionable context for European unification. Throughout the Fouchet Plan negotiations in 1961–62, for instance, Italian representatives acted as chief mediators between the French and the Dutch-Belgian positions. But by the summer of 1962, as the prospect of a Franco-German entente became definite, Italy suddenly stopped playing the role of compromiser and began to champion the Dutch-Belgian position. The sudden change was the result of Italian fears that the entente would undermine the solidity of the Atlantic relationship. The retention of strong Atlantic links was a definite objective, and in its pursuit government leaders were willing to cripple the Fouchet negotiations whose purpose was to promote a political union in Europe — the very goal to which they were so demonstratively committed.

The negotiations between Britain and the EEC during the same period provide another example. The French were intransigent in their insistence that Britain should fully accept the spirit and letter of the Treaty of Rome before it could be admitted to the EEC. In this sense, the French position was in complete accord with Italy's commitment to supranational integration and to the full implementation of the Treaty. Yet, in the course of the negotiations Italy once again tried to act as mediator between the Dutch-Belgian and the French demands. This meant in effect that Italy was willing to accept Britain's entry into the EEC on the basis of concessions that undermined the prospect of genuine regional integration.

The explanation is to be found in the role of "Atlantism" in Italian politics. Italian elites perceived Britain's membership in the EEC as essential to the preservation of close ties between Europe and the USA. Hence the sudden objections to the Fouchet negotiations for a political union, particularly after the French decision to reject the MLF plan had created the impression that the Atlantic link might be weakened as a result. Rhetoric notwithstanding, in practice Italy placed its rigid determination to maintain solid NATO links before its commitment to European unification. Its objections to French EEC policies stemmed from the fear that an autonomous Europe, under French influence, would move away from the Atlantic relationship.[78] In the process, because of its preponderant concern with Atlantism, Italy failed to realize that perhaps the only possible united Europe may well be an autonomous Europe.

Italy's role during the EEC crisis of 1965 provides an illustration *a contrario* of the impact of Atlantism on its behavior towards the European Community. Unlike previous situations in which Italy had tended to be the compromiser par excellence, during the 1965 crisis it took a rigid stand in defense of the EEC achievements and in support of further developments to promote integration. The same attitude should have led to a negative position concerning Britain's admission in 1962-63, or at least an unwillingness to make anti-integrative concessions. But Britain's admission to the EEC was regarded as important in preserving firm links between the USA and a Europe in the process of unification, while the 1965 crisis had no implications for the Atlantic relationship and thus allowed Italy's commitment to genuine regional integration to prevail.

These examples indicate that the fundamental issue regarding Italy and the EEC is not whether the country is sufficiently committed to European integration, but to what extent regional unification can be accomplished without eroding the Atlantic alliance. As has been shown, any potential conflict between the two commitments has led Italy to adhere to the latter even at the cost of seriously weakening the former. Italy's role at the EEC level has also been negatively affected by the pervasive pressure of national economic interests.

Through the late 1960s the record of economic growth and trade relations within the EEC indicates consistent net gains for the Italian economy. Of all member states, Italy registered the greatest increase in intra-EEC exports, as well as in GNP per capita and in industrial growth. During the 1958-69 period, for instance, while the total gain in GNP per capita for all EEC countries was 52%, Italy's was 62%. During the same period, there was an increase in industrial production of 81% for the EEC as a whole, but an increase of 133% for Italy. For the EEC as a whole exports increased by 182%, but almost 300% for Italy. The greatest portion of the expanded Italian exports has gone to EEC countries, and has coincided with a radical change in the pattern of Italian foreign trade from a position of chronic deficit to one of equilibrium.[79] These significant gains, to a considerable extent the result of Italy's membership in the EEC, have been recognized by political and economic elites in Italy. Even within the agricultural sector — where, as influential pressure groups claimed, Italy has been negatively affected by the EEC — actual losses have been minimal as contrasted with Germany and

Belgium. In real trade terms, the vast majority of Italian farmers have generally benefited from the EEC; only a few sectors have been partially harmed as a result of the common agricultural policy.[80]

Whatever negative impact the EEC agricultural policy has had on the Italian economy, moreover, its major cause was the government's failure to bring about the needed structural changes in agriculture. Yet throughout the 1960s, Italian policy within the European Community was dominated by the government's determination to amend the 1962 EEC agricultural agreement so as to derive greater benefits for some sectors of Italian agriculture. The government was responding to domestic pressure groups, but it was also undermining the country's commitment to integration because of the resulting conflicts with other EEC countries.

This became quite apparent during the events that led to the 1965 EEC crisis, when Italy insisted on pursuing economic gains despite the real risk that its demands would aggravate an already difficult situation. In early 1965, the EEC Commission had presented to the Community Council a package proposal linking a new financing project for agriculture to an increase in powers for the European Parliament. While in favor of the political aims of this proposal, Italy demanded that the agreement on financial regulations be postponed until the 1962 EEC agricultural fund had been modified in accordance with Italy's longstanding request. Such a response was marked by a glaring inconsistency which in the end could only harm the prospects for integration. On the one hand, Italy expected the other EEC members to accept the political side of the Commission's proposal (to increase the powers of the European Parliament — the aspect most unwelcome to France), while on the other hand demanding the postponement of the new financing project (which was most urgently needed by France). In fact, Italy's rigid stand was utilized by France as a major reason for breaking off the negotiations with other EEC countries on June 30, 1965.[81]

Germany's attitude provides a revealing contrast to the Italian response. Since 1962, Germany has been the greatest net loser in its transactions with the EEC Agricultural Fund. In the 1962–68 period, for instance, while Germany's losses amounted to 323 million dollars, Italy's were only 11 million. In trade terms, although some sectors of German farming benefited from higher EEC prices, by and large German farmers were negatively affected by regional integration. Dissatisfaction was strong and widespread; the Deutsche Bauern-Verband went as far as to demand a revision of the Treaty of Rome and accused the German government of neglecting the national interest in the name of European unification. Yet, in spite of economic losses and strong domestic objections, the German government did not try to modify its commitment to the EEC agricultural policy with the same uncompromising vehemence as Italy. It was willing to tolerate losses in the agricultural sector, and in its support of integration it showed the determination and ability to withstand powerful domestic pressures demanding a different policy.[82]

The Italian government, on the other hand, seems unable to resist negative domestic pressures, so that commitments cannot be translated into actual policies in accord with the regional process. Both domestically and at the EEC level, Italian responses have tended to serve narrow economic interests. While French responses may be totally nationalistic, from the viewpoint of regional unification the French political system can be counted on to carry out agreements to which it has committed itself. But the Italian government's acceptance of EEC policies provides no assurance of its ability to implement them effectively.

4. CONCLUSION: EUROPEAN UNIFICATION OR ATLANTIC SOLIDARITY?

Si le terrain vous paraît ne pas correspondre aux indications de votre carte d'état-major, soyez certain que c'est le terrain qui a raison.
(Advice of a French general to his officers)[83]

What happens outside a region such as Western Europe, and particularly how it is perceived by the member states, naturally affects the process of regional unification. Since the creation of NATO in 1949, many Italian leaders have perceived the goals of European unity and Atlantic solidarity as mutually reinforcing. Before 1949, however, political leaders of the same parties that would later firmly support the NATO/Europe link regarded the prospect of European unification as an *alternative* to the formation of a military alliance of the NATO type. At that time there was general agreement among virtually all non-communist political groups that Italy ought to join the West as an indispensable condition for reaffirming the country's self-respect and identity. However, it was generally felt that these goals should be realized within a unified Europe, and not through military alliances.[84] Thus the 1948 Brussels Treaty (which set up a military organization linking Britain, France, and the Benelux countries) had been ignored by Italian leaders because they regarded it as an old-fashioned military alliance that could not serve as a starting point for European unification.

Instead, Italian government leaders made a concerted effort to involve other European countries in transforming the Organization for European Economic Cooperation (OEEC) into a political community; it was their belief that a military alliance between Western Europe and the USA would pose a serious threat to the prospect for European unity. An international role for Italy limited to bringing about a united Europe was also perceived as necessary to enable all parties and political groups to minimize their differences and engage in cooperative efforts. On the other hand, it was feared that a military alliance with the USA would divide the country into two hostile and irreconcilable blocs. For all these reasons, Italy's reluctant entry into NATO occurred only after the realization that the hoped-for European community would not rapidly materialize, and under the pressure of international events which virtually removed other options.

Soon this decision was to affect the country's European orientation.

Pro-NATO groups justified their support for Italy's entry into the alliance as essential to promote European unity itself, while the anti-NATO groups argued that the alliance would undermine all prospects for European unification. In effect, the pro-NATO forces subordinated their European ideal to Atlantic solidarity, and convinced themselves that the two goals would be mutually reinforcing. Yet, this was merely an act of faith that was later to contribute to the shallow and contradictory aspects of Italy's response to NATO, as well as to the country's incongruous and harmful behavior towards the European Community. Ultimately, NATO was to become a most divisive force within the Italian political scene, thus contributing to the alienation of the leftist forces from the goal of European unity.[85]

In the original formulation of the theory of European integration in the 1950s, the role of external influences (and NATO specifically) was not given primary importance since the USA was fully committed to European integration and acted as an effective catalyst. In the 1960s, however, the European-Atlantic relationship was singled out as a major factor contributing to the difficulties in achieving European unification. But its impact was analyzed mostly in terms of the controversy among the six members of the EEC that arose from conflicting concepts of the nature of the relationship.[86] In the Italian case, as has been shown, the European-Atlantic relationship exerted additional influence because of NATO's direct link with the very identity and orientation of the Italian political system. As a result, whenever a potential conflict arose between the goal of European unity and the Atlantic commitment, Italy almost automatically opted for the latter. In so doing — aside from policy declarations during the 1950s and 1960s — Italian leaders actually promoted types of policies within the EEC and domestically that were detrimental to the prospects of European political and economic unification. At the same time, while reasserting their original act of faith — that firm Atlantic links would somehow favor European unity as well — Italian leaders did not realize that their EEC policy choices had a negative impact on the regional process.

While a Gaullist vision for a united Europe independent of the USA might easily have mobilized the most significant political forces in Italy before the creation of NATO, by the 1960s it came to be seen as anathema. Italy's resistance to Gaullist policies has been portrayed as a defense of supranational integration; but de Gaulle's Europe would have signified a radical alteration of the status quo away from the Atlantic link, and as such it was perceived as threatening to Italy's political system. To summarize, the preeminence of the Atlantic relationship in Italian eyes has been a major cause of the country's equivocal behavior towards the European Community. First, by perceiving NATO and the EEC as two interrelated processes, Italian leaders tended to approach them in a similar manner, mostly by reasserting their loyalty to both while expecting the integrative process to occur automatically — thus failing to foster the appropriate domestic responses promoting integration. At the Community level this led to Italy's strong support of contradictory developments such as supranationality and Britain's admission to the EEC. Ultimately, in giving priority to the Atlantic relationship Italy's behavior within the European Community helped undermine the only realistic possibility of political union available in the 1960s — de Gaulle's European Europe.

The diplomatic contacts between France and Italy during 1962–64 regarding the political unification of Europe provide a good illustration of the underlying reality of Italy's concerns. It soon became clear that the issues at stake had little to do with the shape of the European Community per se; it was the Atlantic link that mostly concerned the Italian government. At one point this was explicitly recognized by the Italian Foreign Minister when he stated that the various projects for European political unity were not making any progress because Italy feared that, should those projects be realized along French ideas, they would compromise the "visione comunitaria dell'alleanza atlantica." [87] In effect, then, leaving aside the rhetoric of more than two decades, the real issue for Italy within the European Community has not been the conflict between two visions regarding the nature of the integration process (*Europe des Etats* vs. supranational Europe) but the role of the Atlantic relationship within a uniting Europe. This has contributed to the internalization process of EEC and NATO issues, which has prevented Italian parties and governments from regarding the European Community as a type of organization requiring a new kind of response.

Italy's insistence on maintaining firm Atlantic links, in general and in opposition to de Gaulle specifically, has been quite unrelated to NATO's potential contributions to European unification. Although during the 1960s the Atlantic relationship actually had an anti-integrative impact on the EEC, Italian leaders continued to insist on rigid fidelity to NATO as essential to European unification as well as to Italian security. But to oppose France's EEC policies during that period in the name of NATO and security was to ignore the fact that de Gaulle never rejected NATO as a military alliance; he regarded it as indispensable to European security.[88] Moreover, one could argue — and the point has been made by leftist political groups in Italy — that a relaxation of the Atlantic commitment and the creation of a more autonomous Europe would actually enhance European security.

As has been shown, the critical issue was the intricate connection between the Atlantic relationship and the Italian political system. With the advent of the Center-Left coalition in 1962 there was a heightened concern, within the Center parties, to maintain firm Atlantic links. This was necessary to reassure conservative groups that the political system would not lapse from its close identification with the Atlantic Alliance. For other reasons, despite its reservations about NATO, the Socialist party also pressed for the retention of Atlantic links as a way of opposing de Gaulle's European vision.[89]

Thus, during the period when the possibility was emerging for concrete moves towards European political unity through France's Fouchet Plan, Italy could not support it because of its rigid commitment to an Atlantic orientation. Although in 1960 Italy had taken the first active steps in promoting a political union among EEC countries, by 1962 it was to be instrumental in undermining the realization of such a union. It was officially claimed that because of its commitment to supranationality, Italy could not accept the Fouchet Plan since it was basically a project for inter-governmental cooperation; but, in fact, Italy's own 1960 proposal for a political union did not substantially differ from the Fouchet Plan. The real difference was that by 1962, during the most delicate phase in the emergence of the Center-Left government, the Atlantic connection was perceived as indispensable for domestic reasons. Hence Italy insisted on Britain's participation in the Fouchet Plan negotiations as a way to insure the permanence of close American-European ties, although in so doing it helped undermine the negotiations.

By the mid-1960s it was becoming evident, both in Europe and the USA, that the Atlantic Alliance was impeding the regional process.[90] It was also becoming clear that political unity in Europe would not come about automatically and that economic integration itself would not continue unless accompanied, or rather preceded, by a firm political commitment and an agreement on political goals. The Italian case illustrates many of the dynamics involved in these problems. It also points to a serious dilemma which is present, at least in part, in other EEC countries as well. On the one hand, European political unity could be a genuine alternative to the function that the Atlantic relationship has performed for West European states, and for the Italian political system in particular. It might even facilitate the functioning of the Italian system, since a diminution of the Atlantic involvement would enlarge its political base of support among left-wing political parties and factions. On the other hand, the very precariousness of the system and its political-psychological dependence on the Atlantic link has prevented the emergence of a political will capable of accepting and promoting a European union which would involve a loosening of the NATO ties. Yet, this kind of united Europe may well be the only feasible one.

The dynamics of the political system also negatively affect Italy's integrative behavior both nationally and at the EEC level. As has been shown, the precariousness of the political system reinforces the tendency towards the internalization of NATO and EEC issues and accounts for the limited political significance of the European Community within Italy. This process also contributes to the resistance of parties and governments to integrative pressures, despite their commitment to regional unification. In other words, the major obstacle to integrative responses is not to be found in the parties per se, but in the functioning of the political system that compels parties, in actual behavior if not in policy declarations, to ignore their European commitment.

In its original formulation, the neo-functionalist theory of European integration had assumed that a positive commitment to the regional process by various political and economic groups within a country would almost automatically generate integrative behavior. By the late 1960s, the revised theory indicated that the political-social structures of the "New Europe" were no longer sufficient to guarantee continued integration, and that in fact the domestic political situation in various countries constituted a critical variable. However, there was no explicit recognition of the possibility that the dynamics of a certain political system, like Italy's, could in themselves negatively affect the integrative process. The failure to recognize this new variable may result partly from the assumption of the neo-functionalist theorists that all EEC countries correspond to the model of a technocratic-pluralist system in which "political parties and interest groups avoid sharp ideological conflicts." [91] The behavior of parties and the resulting stalemating tendencies of the Italian political system are, to a large extent, due to intense ideological divisions in the country. The technocratic-pluralist model is not sufficiently applicable to the Italian situation; the ideological debate does affect the parties' integrative responses. Thus a weak and stalemated system can undermine integrative pressures despite widespread commitment in favor of regional unification. As Karl Deutsch has indicated, dysfunctional developments (e.g., rigidity) within a political system may negatively affect its functioning, including the system's ability to modify itself and to learn new patterns of behavior.[92] The resulting stagnation in these situations actually renders the system impenetrable to pressures for change. This type of system can in effect defy the semi-automatic and presumably irresistible dynamics of the neo-functionalist regional process.

The Italian case confirms the importance of the factors that were being emphasized in the revised theory of European integration in the

1960s — the national political situation in the countries involved in the regional process, and the impact of extra-regional links such as the Atlantic Alliance. Some scholars have long insisted that the slowing down of European unification during the 1960s was only marginally related to Gaullist policies. Italy's behavior towards the EEC and its negative interactions with French policies provide support for this conclusion. Writing from the perspective of 1970, Joseph Nye concluded that inertia will be the "normal" tendency in the regional and national behavior of decision-makers concerning integration, "as long as the process forces or popular pressures are not so strong as to make this choice unbearable for them." [93]

The Italian case indicates that the nature of the political system itself represents a critical variable. Apart from the role of extra-regional factors, strong group pressures and intense mass opinion within each country may not suffice in promoting integrative behavior, unless there is also a political system capable of translating those pressures into effective policy and capable of responding to integrative dynamics at the regional level. A solid political system like that of the French Fifth Republic may effectively resist integrative pressures because of the anti-integrative will of its leaders. A weak political system like that of Italy can substantially minimize the effect of integrative pressures because of the dynamics generated by its own precariousness, and despite the leaders' commitment to integration. In the contemporary process of regional unification, weak and powerful political systems can bring about similar results.

NOTES

1. James N. Rosenau, ed., *Linkage Politics* (New York, Free Press, 1969), pp. 2, 5.
2. See, for example, R. Barry Farrell, ed., *Approaches to Comparative and International Politics* (Evanston, Northwestern University Press, 1966); also Edward L. Morse, "The Transformation of Foreign Policies," *World Politics*, April 1970.
3. See the following for a representative sample: Leon N. Lindberg, *The Political Dynamics of European Economic Integration* (Stanford, Stanford University Press, 1963); Stephen R. Graubard, ed., *A New Europe?* (Boston, Houghton Mifflin, 1964); Stanley Hoffmann, "Obstinate or Obsolete? The Fate of the Nation-State and the Case of Western Europe," *Daedalus*, Summer 1966; Karl W. Deutsch, *et al.*, *France, Germany and the Western Alliance* (New York, Charles Scribner's Sons, 1967); Leon N. Lindberg, "Integration as a Source of Stress on the European Community System," *International Organization*, Spring 1966; G. L. Weil, "European Community: What Lies Beyond the Point of No Return?", *Review of Politics*, April 1967; Amitai Etzioni, *Political Unification* (New York, Holt, Rinehart and Winston, 1965); Ernst Haas, *"The Uniting of Europe* and the Uniting of Latin America," *Journal of Common Market Studies*, June 1967. See also various articles in the periodical *Government and Opposition*, April–July 1967.
4. See, for instance, Ernst van der Beugel, *From Marshall Aid to Atlantic Partnership* (Amsterdam, Elsevier, 1966); F. A. M. Alting von Gesau, *European Organisation and Foreign Relations of States* (Leiden, A. W. Sijthoff, 1962); Timothy W. Stanley, *NATO in Transition* (New York, Praeger, 1965). Specific country studies tend to be either very vague and polemical or strictly legalistic; see, for instance, Institut Royal des Relations Internationales, *Les Conséquences d'Ordre Interne de la Participation de la Belgique aux Organisations Internationales* (Brussels, 1964); Riccardo Monaco, *Diritto delle Comunità Europee e Diritto Interno* (Milan, Giuffré, 1967).
5. See, for example, Karl Kaiser, "The US and the EEC in the Atlantic System: The Problem of Theory," *Journal of Common Market Studies*, June 1967; Leon N. Lindberg and Stuart A. Scheingold, *Europe's Would-Be Polity* (Englewood Cliffs, Prentice-Hall, 1970); L. B. Krause, ed., *The Common Market* (Englewood Cliffs, Prentice-Hall, 1964); R. W. Cox, "The Study of European Institutions; Some Problems of Economic and Political Organization," *Journal of Common Market Studies*, February 1965; James N. Rosenau, *Of Boundaries and Bridges* (Princeton, Center for International Studies, January 1967). The importance of differing national situations was already being stressed in the early 1960s by Stanley Hoffmann; see, for instance, his "Discord in Community: The North Atlantic Area as a Partial International System" in Francis O. Wilcox, ed., *The Atlantic Community* (New York, Praeger, 1963). A later study emphasizing the same dynamics is Joseph S. Nye, *Peace in Parts: Integration and Conflict in Regional Organization* (Boston, Little, Brown, 1971).
6. See, for instance, G. P. Orsello, ed., *L'Italia e L'Europa* (Rome, Edizione Abete, 1966); Gaetano Martino, *et al.*, *Traguardo Europa* (Florence, Vallecchi, 1966); Bino Olivi, *L'Europa Difficile* (Milan, Comunità, 1964); Paolo

Taviani, *Solidarietà Atlantica e Comunità Europea* (Florence, Le Monnier, 1967); Vittorio Orilia, *Imperialismo Atlantico* (Padua, Marsilio, 1969); Istituto Affari Internazionali, *La Politica Estera della Repubblica Italiana* (Milan, Comunità, 1967); Giovanni di Capua, et al., *Che Fare della NATO?* (Florence, Editrice Politica, 1967); P. A. Milani, ed., *La NATO: Problemi e Prospettive* (Milan, Giuffré, 1967); Luigi Graziano, *La Politica Estera Italiana nel Dopoguerra* (Padua, Marsilio, 1968).

7. For further details on the dynamics of the Italian political system, see Giorgio Galli, *Il Bipartitismo Imperfetto* (Bologna, Il Mulino, 1966); Joseph La Palombara, *Interest Groups in Italian Politics* (Princeton, Princeton University Press, 1964); Dante Germino and Stefano Passigli, *The Government and Politics of Contemporary Italy* (New York, Harper, 1968); Mattei Dogan and Orazio Petracca, *Partiti Politici e Strutture Sociali in Italia* (Milan, Comunità, 1968); Norman Kogan, *The Government of Italy* (New York, Praeger, 1962); Joseph La Palombara, ed., *Political Parties and Development* (Princeton, Princeton University Press, 1966); Istituto di Studi e Ricerche C. Cattaneo, *Ricerche Sulla Partecipazione Politica in Italia* (four volumes published by Il Mulino, Bologna, 1967, 1968, 1969).

8. Stanley Hoffmann et al., *In Search of France* (Cambridge, Mass., Harvard University Press, 1963), p. 2.

9. For an illustration, see speeches by government leaders and spokesmen of various parties during parliamentary debates in the late 1940s, 1950s, or 1960s (e.g., Camera dei Deputati, *Atti Parlamentari*, July 1949, October 1968).

10. See the following official and unofficial Christian Democratic publications: *Cronache Sociali, Politica d'Oggi, Libertà, Popolo, Politica Sociale*, for the 1948–49 period. The politically independent newspaper *Corriere della Sera* of the same period provides additional details and confirmation. See also the parliamentary records, particularly for the following dates: *Atti Parlamentari*, November–December 1948; March 13–20, 1949. See also Carlo Falconi, *I Papi del Ventesimo Secolo* (Milan, Feltrinelli, 1967); Giorgio Gualerzi, *La Politica Estera dei Popolari* (Rome, Cinque Lune, 1959); Domenico Settembrini, *La Chiesa Nella Politica Estera Italiana* (Pisa, Nistri, 1964); Mario Cocchi, *La Sinistra Cattolica e la Resistenza* (Rome, Edizioni Internazionali, 1966); Luigi Sturzo, *Il Partito Popolare Italiano* (Bologna, Zanichelli, 1956); Giorgio Galli and Paolo Facchi, *La Sinistra Democristiana* (Milan, Feltrinelli, 1962). Prime Minister de Gasperi, afraid of domestic repercussions, was then reluctant to bring Italy into the Atlantic Alliance; see Paolo Canali, *Alcide De Gasperi nella Politica Estera Italiana* (Milan, Mondadori, 1953); Alberto Tarchiani, *Dieci Anni tra Roma e Washington* (Milan, Mondadori, 1955). Foreign Minister Carlo Sforza was also a reluctant advocate of Italy's membership in NATO and favored a process of European unification instead; see his *Cinque Anni a Palazzo Chigi* (Rome, Atlante, 1952). Both leaders eventually felt that the hope of a united Europe was waning and that isolation would be harmful to Italy's security and political autonomy. See, for instance, de Gasperi's speeches in *Atti Parlamentari*, March 11–17, 1949; also Sforza, *op. cit.*, chapters 9 and 10. Similar reactions and views are found in Konrad Adenauer, *Memoirs* (Chicago, Regnery, 1966). Left-wing Christian Democratic spokesmen, however, felt that NATO was mostly being used to influence the shape of the domestic political system; and their views had not changed by the 1960s. See, for instance, Luigi Gui's speech in Democrazia Cristiana, *Convegno di San Pellegrino* (Vol. I, Rome, 1964), p. 385; see also *Politica*, May 1, 1965; *Nuovo Osservatore*, No. 64, 1967.

11. In later years the distinction between the Social Democratic and the orthodox Christian Democratic position on NATO disappeared. But in 1948–49 the differences were real and profound. See, for instance, *Umanità*, March 18, 1949. At the January 1949 Social Democratic party congress, the pro-NATO

resolution only obtained 49% of the vote; at a meeting of the party directorate on the eve of the NATO vote in parliament, the neutralist faction obtained a majority. See *Umanità*, February–March 1949; PSLI, *Atti del Secondo Congresso* (Rome, 1949). *Umanità*, the party newspaper, continued to oppose NATO through the spring of 1949. The majority of the Social Democrats condemned NATO as a reactionary scheme by anti-socialist groups; they also felt that NATO would signify the end of prospects for European unification, which they regarded as the best way for Europe to play a meaningful role by acting as mediator between East and West. See, for instance, speeches by Mario Zagari and Rodolfo Mondolfo: *Atti Parlamentari*, December 1, 4, 1948; March 11–17, 1949. Giuseppe Saragat himself had justified the 1947 decision to join the government coalition as indispensable to avoid the formation of a right-wing government. See *Umanità*, January 19, 1947, and December 14, 1947; also G. Saragat, *Quaranta Anni di Lotta per la Democrazia* (Milano, Mursia, 1966).

12. During 1948–49, PSI leaders tried to move the country towards neutrality; they argued that Italy was not threatened by a foreign country, and that NATO was in effect intended to influence the domestic political situation — to become an instrument of conservatism, like the 19th century Holy Alliance. See *Atti Parlamentari*, November 30, 1948, March and July 1949; *Corriere della Sera* and *Avanti*, 1948–49, *passim*; Pietro Nenni, *Il Cappio delle Alleanze* (Florence, Parenti, 1949); also his *Dal Patto Atlantico alla Distensione* (Florence, Parenti, 1953).

13. In 1946, before the split into two socialist parties, the Socialist party (PSI) had obtained 20.7% of the vote (as compared with 18.9% for the Communists and 35% for the Christian Democrats). The potential existed for a single semi-autonomous socialist party to exert great influence. Regarding the links between the Socialists and the Communists, even a Christian Democratic leader — Dino del Bo — has acknowledged that the PSI's neutralist foreign policy was not due to its ties with the PCI; see his *La Convivenza degli Italiani* (Milan, Garzanti, 1959). See also Mario Einaudi, *et al.*, *Communism in Western Europe* (Ithaca, Cornell University Press, 1951); *Voce Repubblicana*, April 5, 1948; *Atti Parlamentari*, March 1, 1948, July 19, 1949; PSI, *28 Congresso Nazionale* (1949); PSLI, *I Congresso Nazionale* (1948), and *Congresso Straordinario* (June 1949).

14. See views expressed during parliamentary debates on the Treaty of Rome; Camera dei Deputati, *Discussioni*, July 1957; Senato, *Resoconti*, October 1957. See also Democrazia Cristiana, *Atti e Documenti: 1943–69* (Rome, 1969); article by A. Fanfani in *Il Popolo*, August 4, 1957; G. Martino, *Verso l'Avvenire* (Florence, Le Monnier, 1963); L. Graziano, *La Politica Estera Italiana nel Dopoguerra* (Padua, Marsilio, 1968).

15. These conclusions refer to the party majority; there was also a vocal minority that vehemently opposed the EEC, regarding it as a tool of conservative forces. See speeches by Lombardi and Basso, Camera dei Deputati, *Discussioni*, July 1957. For details on the party as a whole, see *Avanti*, July 20, 1957; PSI, *32 Congresso Nazionale* (1957); P. Nenni, *Il Socialismo nella Democrazia* (Florence, Vallecchi, 1966).

16. The Soviet position had great impact on the PCI. Thus, for instance, the lead editorial in *Unità* of January 29, 1957 extended a wary welcome to the EEC; but two weeks later, after the Soviets had openly condemned the EEC, the PCI reversed its position. See Senato, *Resoconti*, February 13–15, 1957. See also G. Pajetta, *Perchè il PCI è contro il Mercato Comune* (Rome, SETI, 1957).

17. The groups in favor of Center-Left coalition focused on the Socialist party's stand concerning the European Community as an indication of a definite turning point in PCI–PSI relations and as an incentive to accelerate the moves

towards an entente with the Socialists. On the other hand, the groups opposed to the Center-Left plan tried to capitalize on the ambiguities in the Socialist position to undermine that plan. See *Corriere della Sera*, March–November 1957; PSI, *32 Congresso Nazionale* (Rome, 1957); see also reports and exchanges among various factions in the Socialist party press, e.g. *Avanti*, 1957, *passim*. By 1957 the leaders of the Social Democratic party had come to regard the links between the PSI and the PCI as the only insurmountable obstacle to a reunification of the two socialist parties and to their collaboration in a government coalition with the DC. For this reason, the Social Democrats regarded the Treaty of Rome as an opportunity to test the responses of the PSI. See *Giustizia*, February 2, 1957; *Popolo*, April 3, 1957.
18. The crisis and downfall of the Segni cabinet in May 1957 was related to this confrontation within the party. See *Popolo*, April–July 1957; see also debates at the DC party executive's meeting of February 1957, reported in *Popolo*, February 6, 1957. For the Liberal party's position see Malagodi's presentation in parliament: Camera, *Discussioni*, July 20, 1957. For opposing views within the DC, see coverage in *Avanti*, 1957, *passim*.
19. See coverage of the CGIL position in *Unità* of July 22, 1957. See also Giorgio Galli, "La Politica Internazionale del Partito Comunista Italiano," in Istituto Affari Internazionali, *La Politica Estera . . . op. cit.*; Donald Blackmer, *Unity in Diversity: Italian Communism and the Communist World* (Cambridge, Mass., MIT Press, 1967); Pietro Nenni, *Una Legislatura Fallita* (Milan, Edizioni Avanti, 1958); Quaderni del Centro la Nuova Guida, *Integrazione Economica e Unità Politica dell'Europa* (Rome, 1963); *Mondo Operaio*, 1957, *passim*.
20. In 1951–52, against the growing pressure from the Right and the extreme Left, de Gasperi himself had revived this vision and hope. See Alcide de Gasperi, *Per L'Europa* (Rome, Cinque Lune, 1952).
21. See A. Chiti-Batelli, "Il Piano Fouchet o del Fallimento dei Progetti di Unione Politica Europea," in L. S. Olschki, *La Comunità Europea* (Florence, La Colombaria, 1969); Alessandro Silj, *Europe's Political Puzzle* (Cambridge, Mass., Harvard University Center for International Affairs, 1967); Miriam Camps, *European Unification in the Sixties* (New York, McGraw-Hill, 1966); Achille Albonetti, *Preistoria degli Stati Uniti d'Europa* (Milan, Giuffré, 1964).
22. See, for example, *Corriere della Sera*, April 18, 1962; also the pro-government publication *Relazioni Internazionali*, April 28, 1962.
23. The gravity of the situation was epitomized in an editorial in *Relazioni Internazionali*, June 23, 1962, which concluded that the crisis within the European Community had reached a stage at which it could seriously undermine and destroy the entire process of European unification.
24. This lack of response and attention persisted even during debates specifically devoted to foreign affairs, both in Parliament and within the parties. See *Popolo, Avanti, Giustizia, Voce Repubblicana*, June-December 1962; Camera dei Deputati, *Discussioni*, and Senato, *Resoconti*, for the same period; Democrazia Cristiana, *Atti e Documenti*, 1959–69.
25. See, for instance, the EEC-sponsored conference held in Rome at the end of December 1962, which was attended by leading politicians and by journalists of all major publications.
26. See Camera dei Deputati, *Discussioni*, January-June 1963; *Avanti, Popolo, Giustizia* for the same period; Democrazia Cristiana, *9 Congresso Nazionale* (Rome, 1964).
27. See Presidenza del Consiglio dei Ministri, *L'Italia e L'Integrazione Europea* (Rome, 1964); semi-official reports in *Esteri*, 1963; *European Documentation*, March 1963.
28. Camps, *European Unification . . . , op. cit.*, p. 29.
29. On the government side as well there was little indication of concern with

the issues beyond a mere reassertion of a vague commitment to integration. See, for instance, reports and speeches by Foreign Minister Fanfani: Camera dei Deputati, *Discussioni* and Senato, *Resoconti*, January-June 1965, *passim*. See also reports in *La Stampa, Corriere della Sera, Relazioni Internazionali*, July-October 1965. For President de Gaulle's position, see *Le Monde*, September 11, 1965. See also John Newhouse, *Collision in Brussels* (New York, Norton, 1967).

30. See, for instance, *Avanti*, July 3, 1965; *Vita*, October 5, 1965; *Giustizia*, July 15, 1965; *Il Centro*, September 15, 1965; *Popolo*, October 9, 1965; Partito Socialista Italiano, *36 Congresso Nazionale del PSI* (Rome, 1965).
31. Camera dei Deputati, *Discussioni*, 1958-70; Senato, *Resoconti*, 1958-70.
32. Senato, *Commissione Esteri*, February 13, 1963. The same pattern appeared at subsequent meetings of this committee as well as in general debates.
33. James N. Rosenau, "Pre-theories and Theories of Foreign Policy," in Farrell, *Approaches . . .* , *op. cit.*, p. 65. See also Karl W. Deutsch, "External Influences on the Internal Behavior of States," in Farrell; E. L. Morse, "The Transformation of Foreign Policies," *World Politics*, April 1970.
34. See, for instance, the DC left-wing publication *Politica*, especially the issue of November 1, 1965; Democrazia Cristiana, *Atti del IX Congresso* (Rome, 1964); Piero Ostellino, *L'Italia tra Atlantismo e Neutralismo* (Turin, Centro Ricerca Einaudi, 1964); E. Ceccarini et al., *La NATO nell'Era della Distensione* (Bologna, Il Mulino, 1966); Democrazia Cristiana, *Atti e Documenti della DC* (Rome, 1968); *Politica Estera*, June 1965; Partito Liberale Italiano, *Azione Politica e Legislativa del PLI, 1963-65* (Rome, 1965). This pattern was also explicitly recognized by party leaders; see, for instance, speech by Fanfani, in March 1962, in which he openly accused the right-wing factions and parties of utilizing issues of defense as a façade for their opposition to the social and economic aspects of the government coalition: Senato, *Resoconti*, March 12-25, 1962. See also similar assertions by Saragat in *Giustizia*, January 7, 1962; and by Nenni in *Avanti*, September 5, 1965. For details on the MLF, see Alastair Buchan, "The MLF: an Historical Perspective," *Adelphi Papers*, October 1964.
35. Even the general press recognized the implications of those EEC crises. See for example, *Corriere della Sera* and *Messaggero*, January-February 1963 and July 1965. For the domestic dimensions of the EEC developments, see views expressed by Christian Democrats and Liberals: Senato, *Resoconti*, March-July 1962; Camera dei Deputati, *Discussioni*, October 9-11, 1963 and March 5, 1964; Democrazia Cristiana, *VIII Congresso Nazionale* (Rome, 1962), and *IX Congresso Nazionale* (Rome, 1964); *Idea Liberale*, No. 3, 1959; *Nord-Sud*, No. 55, 1959.
36. OECD, *National Accounts Statistics*, 1950-70; United Nations, *Yearbook of National Accounts Statistics*, 1969.
37. See declarations by Defense Minister Roberto Tremelloni in Camera dei Deputati, *Commissione Difesa*, November 10, 1966. See also Camera dei Deputati, *Repertorio dei Lavori Legislativi* (III, IV, V Legislatura); Senato, *Commissione Difesa* (1958-63, 1963-68); *Spettatore Internazionale*, No. 4, 1967. Documentation related to these questions is also regularly reprinted in *Relazioni Internazionali* and *Annuario Internazionale* (ISPI, Milan).
38. See, for instance, debates in the Senate Foreign Affairs Committee on the missile bases: Senato, *Commissione Esteri*, January 23, 1958. Another indication of the same attitude was the reaction to the American decision to remove the missiles in the early 1960s, which was perceived as a loss of status in Italy. See, for instance, reports in *Corriere della Sera*, 1962-63, *passim*. Hence also the consistent Italian emphasis on converting NATO from a military to a political community. See, for example, Giovanni Gronchi, *Discorsi d'America* (Milan, Garzanti, 1956).
39. P. Luzzato Fegiz, *Il Volto Sconosciuto dell'Italia* (Milan, Guiffré, 1966);

R. L. Merrit and D. J. Puchala, eds., *Western European Perspectives on International Affairs* (New York, Praeger, 1968).

40. See, for instance, *Critica Marxista*, May 1966, March 1968, January 1969, and *Il Confronto*, January 1967, for an expression of Communist views. For Socialist views, see *Mondo Operaio*, April 1969.
41. By the mid-1960s, for instance, many DC groups were explicitly asking for radical revisions in the alliance. See *Politica*, September 1, 1968; *Nuovo Osservatore*, No. 65, 1967. The official party position has also changed; for instance, by 1969, the new DC secretary was stating that conditions were ripe for a "new conception of the Atlantic Alliance, for a more political and more open role moving towards a serious dialogue between East and West." See *Popolo*, November 8, 1969.
42. See Gronchi, *Discorsi . . . op. cit.*: Amintore Fanfani, *La DC e i Problemi Internazionali* (Rome, Cinque Lune, 1957) and *Dopo Firenze* (Milan, Garzanti, 1961); *Politica*, May 1, 1965, March 15, 1966; *Quest'Italia*, May 1969.
43. See Pietro Nenni, *Dal Patto Atlantico alla Politica di Distensione* (Florence, Parenti, 1953); Palmiro Togliatti, *Per Salvaguardare e Consolidare la Pace* (Rome, Editori Riuniti, 1961); Giovanni Gronchi, *Una Politica Sociale* (Bologna, Il Mulino, 1962); Democrazia Cristiana, *La DC di Fronte all'Avvenire* (Rome, Cinque Lune, 1964).
44. See, for instance, statement by the DC party leader on NATO and relations with the Communist party: *Popolo*, November 8, 1969.
45. See *Civitas, Il Centro, La Discussione, Politica, Popolo*, August–November 1968. As late as 1969, conservative forces were to invoke the NATO symbolism and the unsettled conditions of the early postwar period to resist further leftward trends in domestic politics; in fact, some conservative groups even claimed that NATO was essential to provide protection against the domestic "fifth column" of the Communist party, as in *Rivista Aeronautica*, February 1969.
46. See, for instance, the parliamentary motion of October 1968 calling for Italy's unilateral implementation of direct elections. This motion was supported by all major parties with the exception of the extreme Left: Camera dei Deputati, *Discussioni*, October 7, 1968.
47. The first representative slate of delegates from Italy was elected in 1969. The fact that the PCI was finally included in the Italian delegation invalidates the justifications previously given (that the Communists should not be included because of their opposition to European unification); the real issue was the domestic political struggle. For details on Communist orientations, see *Critica Sociale*, January 5, 1966; *Unità*, May 6, 1966; *Common Market*, April 1969; *Agenor*, June 1969; W. Feld, "French and Italian Communists and the Common Market," *Journal of Common Market Studies*, March 1968.
48. See *Sole-24 Ore*, 1968; *Spettatore Internazionale*, No. 3, 1969; *L'Europa*, Nos. 17, 21, 1969; *Agence Europe, European Documentation, European Community, L'Italia nel MEC*, 1962–70 passim. For many years Italy had been accused by other EEC members of providing indirect export subsidies through its fiscal system, in direct contrast with the provisions and the spirit of the Treaty of Rome. Thus Italy's prompt adoption of the VAT system would have provided an indication of the government's willingness to dispel those accusations. In fact, articles in major business publications argued that the government was doing a disservice to Italian industry by its failure to implement the new EEC regulations. See *Mondo Economico*, May 1969; *Common Market*, No. 3, 1968; *Esteri*, August 31, 1967.
49. For instance, in a case involving Italy's nationalized electric industry, the government argued that the European Community lacked the jurisdiction to decide whether or not Italy's nationalization act was legal from the point of view of the Treaty of Rome. This position, of course, totally rejects the

notion of a Community law. Significantly, there was no reason for Italy to argue the case in this manner since the Treaty of Rome does not exclude the right to nationalize certain industries.
50. See Ministero del Bilancio, *Programma di Sviluppo Economico per il Quinquennio 1965-69* (Rome, 1965). For an elaboration on the preparation and politics of the plan, see Joseph La Palombara, *The Politics of Economic Planning in Italy* (Syracuse, Maxwell School of Public Affairs, 1965).
51. See, for instance, statements by government and party leaders in Parliament: Camera dei Deputati, *Commissione Esteri*, April 7, 1967; *Popolo*, November 29, 1968.
52. See text in *Relazioni Internazionali*, October 1966.
53. See Lawrence Scheinman, "Some Preliminary Notes on Bureaucratic Relationships in the European Economic Community," *International Organization*, Autumn 1966.
54. See, for instance, reports in *La Nazione*, January 1967; *Corriere della Sera*, September 7, 1969; *L'Europa*, 1968-70, *passim*. See also Altiero Spinelli, *The Eurocrats* (Baltimore, Johns Hopkins University Press, 1966); Presidenza del Consiglio dei Ministri, *L'Italia e L'Integrazione Europea* (Rome, 1964).
55. See Istituto Studi Legislativi, *Indagine Sulla Diplomazia Italiana* (Milan, ISLE, 1964); M. M. Olivetti, "La Préparation de la Décision Communautaire au Niveau National Italien," in Pierre Gerbet and Daniel Pepy, *La Décision Dans les Communautés Européennes* (Brussels, Presses Universitaires, 1969).
56. See, for instance, Ernst Haas, *Uniting of Europe* (Stanford, Stanford University Press, 1968).
57. See, for instance, Democrazia Cristiana, *X Congresso Nazionale* (Rome, Spes, 1968); *Popolo*, October 9, 1965.
58. See Democrazia Cristiana, *Atti e Documenti 1943-67*, pp. 1938-2028 (Rome, 1968), *Popolo*, 1960-70, *passim*. See also *Politica* and *Il Centro* of the same period for left-wing and right-wing views respectively.
59. See *Corrispondenza Socialista*, July 1969; *Argomenti Socialisti*, 1965-68, *passim*.
60. See Pietro Nenni, *Il Socialismo Nella Democrazia* (Florence, Vallecchi, 1966); A. Benzoni and V. Tedesco, *Documenti del Socialismo Italiano, 1943-1966* (Padua, Marsilio, 1968); Liliano Faenza, *La Crisi del Socialismo in Italia* (Bologna, Alfa, 1967); *Argomenti Socialisti*, June 1965; *Mondo Operaio*, April 1963, February 1965, September 1966; M. Ferri, *Socialisti in Parlamento* (Milan, Lerici, 1966).
61. See, for instance, *La Giustizia*, January 4, 1962; Senato, *Resoconti*, July 10-11, 1962; *La Voce Repubblicana*, January 1963, *passim*.
62. *Unità*, November 7, 1965. See also Partito Comunista Italiano, "Il PCI sui Problemi della CEE," *Bollettino CESPE*, No. 8, 1967.
63. See, for instance, Partito Comunista Italiano, *L'Integrazione Economica Europea e il Movimento Operaio* (Rome, PCI, 1962) and *XI Congresso Nazionale* (Rome, PCI, 1966); *Foreign Bulletin of the Italian Communist Party*, No. 3, 1963, and No. 2, 1966; Palmiro Togliatti, *Nella Democrazia e nella Pace verso il Socialismo* (Rome, Editori Riuniti, 1963); *Bollettino CESPE*, No. 16, 1968. The party has also influenced the CGIL, which in turn has helped shape the attitude of workers towards European integration. Writing in the early 1960s, Roy Pryce concluded — in *The Political Future of European Unity* (London, Marshband, 1962) — that the combined impact of NATO and the EEC would reduce the influence of the Communist party. The reverse has occurred; and, in fact, by the end of the decade the PCI had become so influential as to cause serious concern at the EEC level. See, for instance, *Common Market*, April 1969, pp. 76-79; *Agenor*, June 1969, pp. 51-55.
64. Some commentators have presumed the existence of an integrative will from

the frequency and intensity of assertions in favor of regional unification. See, for example, L. Levi-Sandri, "Le Marché Commun et l'Italie" (Brussels, EEC, 1967).
65. Haas, *Uniting Europe, op. cit.*, p. xiii.
66. Nye, *Peace in Parts, op. cit.*, Chapter 7.
67. For instance, Lindberg and Scheingold, *Europe's Would-Be Polity, op. cit.*, Chapter 2; Jacques-René Rabier, *Opinion Publique et L'Europe* (Brussels, Institute of Sociology, 1967).
68. See Elio Rogati, "L'Influenza dei Federalisti sulla Politica Europea dell'Italia," in Istituto Affari Internazionali, *La Politica . . . op. cit.*
69. For details on electoral patterns, see A. Spreafico and J. La Palombara, *Elezioni e Comportamento Politico in Italia* (Milan, Comunitá, 1963); Mattei Dogan and O. M. Petracca, *Partiti Politici e Strutture Sociali in Italia* (Milan, Comunitá, 1968); Istituto C. Cattaneo, *Ricerche . . . op. cit.*
70. See survey reported in *L'Europa*, October 20, 1969. See also Rabier, *Opinion Publique . . . op. cit.*; Fegiz, *Il Volto . . . op. cit.*, Vol. II; Merrit and Puchala, *Western European Perspective, op. cit.*
71. See, for example, statements by leaders of Confindustria and Confagricoltura: *24 Ore*, May 26, 1965; *Sole*, May 15, 1969.
72. See, for instance, *Critica Sociale*, January 5, 1966; *Tribuna Sindacale*, February 29, 1968; *Avanti*, April 3, 1968; *European Documentation*, No. 2, 1968, and No. 2, 1969.
73. See A. Korbonski, "The Evolution of COMECON" in *International Political Communities: An Anthology* (New York, Doubleday, 1966).
74. See, for instance, Hoffmann, "Obstinate or Obsolete?" *op. cit.*
75. See Camera dei Deputati, *Discussioni*, June 16-21, 1966. While recognizing the urgent need for structural reforms, the government and parties have been unable to counteract the influence of these conservative groups.
76. For further details on the bureaucratic structure, see Istituto Studi Legislativi, *Indagine . . . op. cit.*; articles by Pietro Quaroni, Fabrizio de Benedetti, and Roberto Aliboni in Istituto Affari Internazionali, *La Politica . . . op. cit.*; Olivetti, "La Préparation . . . *op. cit.*; F. Demarchi, "Una Ricerca Sociologica sulla Burocrazia Centrale," *Rassegna Italiana di Sociologia*, No. 3, 1965; F. Ferrarotti, *Sociologia e Centri di Potere in Italia* (Bari, Laterza, 1962); D. Bartoli, *L'Italia Burocratica* (Milan, Garzanti, 1965); J. La Palombara, *Interest Groups in Italian Politics* (Princeton, Princeton University Press, 1964); A. Cavallari, *Il Potere in Italia* (Milan, Mondadori, 1967).
77. Adenauer, *Memoirs, op. cit.*; de Gasperi, *Per L'Europa, op. cit.*
78. See, for instance, statements by Prime Minister Aldo Moro, Camera dei Deputati, *Discussioni*, March 12, 1965. Basically, Italy's official concern regarding Britain's admission to the EEC resembled the American view on the same issue; that is, that Britain's membership was essential to the permanence of an Atlantic orientation for Europe. See van der Beugel, *From Marshall Aid . . . op. cit.*
79. Statistical Office of the European Communities, *Basic Statistics of the Community* (Brussels, 1970); L. B. Krause, *European Economic Integration and the United States* (Washington, Brookings Institution, 1968).
80. See *Foreign Agricultural Report* (Washington, Economic Research Service, U.S. Department of Agriculture), No. 55, October 1969.
81. For further details, see Camps, *European Unification . . . op. cit.*; Newhouse, *Collision . . . op. cit.*
82. See Carl J. Friedrich, *Europe: An Emergent Nation* (New York, Harper, 1969); Robert van Schaik, *Agriculture in the EEC* (unpublished ms., Center for International Affairs, Harvard University, Cambridge, Mass., 1970); "L'Agriculture Européenne a un Tournant," *Revue du Marché Commun*, December 1969.

83. Source unknown.
84. See, for instance, Prime Minister de Gasperi's attempts, prior to 1949, to promote European unity instead of military alliances. Sforza, *Cinque Anni . . . op. cit.*; Mario Toscano, "Negoziati per la Partecipazione dell'Italia al Patto Atlantico," in Mario Toscano, ed., *Pagine di Storia Contemporanea* (Milan, Giuffré, 1963).
85. See Chapter 1.
86. See Karl Kaiser, "The US and the EEC . . . *op. cit.*; Stanley Hoffmann, *Gulliver's Troubles, Or the Setting of American Foreign Policy* (New York, McGraw-Hill, 1968); A. B. Overstreet, "The Nature and Prospects of European Institutions," *Journal of Common Market Studies,* February 1965.
87. Complete text in *Relazioni Internazionali,* February 29, 1964.
88. See Stanley Hoffmann, "De Gaulle, Europe, and the Atlantic Alliance," *International Organization,* Winter 1964.
89. While committed to an autonomous Europe, the Socialist party was obsessed by the fear of a united Europe dominated by Gaullism which would minimize the influence of socialist forces. Hence the party's campaign in support of Britain's admission together with the Scandinavian countries, as a way of counteracting the Gaullist impact. See *Avanti,* 1964–65, *passim.*
90. See, for instance, Stanley Hoffmann, "The European Process at Atlantic Crosspurposes," *Journal of Common Market Studies,* February 1965.
91. See, for example, Ernst Haas, "*The Uniting of Europe* and the Uniting of Latin America," *Journal of Common Market Studies,* June 1967.
92. Karl W. Deutsch, *The Nerves of Government* (New York, Free Press, 1966), Chapter 13.
93. Nye, *Peace in Parts, op. cit.,* p. 57.

BOOKS WRITTEN UNDER CENTER AUSPICES

BOOKS

The Soviet Bloc, by Zbigniew K. Brzezinski (sponsored jointly with the Russian Research Center), 1960, Harvard University Press. Revised edition, 1967.
The Necessity for Choice, by Henry A. Kissinger, 1961. Harper & Bros.
Strategy and Arms Control, by Thomas C. Schelling and Morton H. Halperin, 1961. Twentieth Century Fund.
United States Manufacturing Investment in Brazil, by Lincoln Gordon and Engelbert L. Grommers, 1962. Harvard Business School.
The Economy of Cyprus, by A. J. Meyer, with Simos Vassiliou (sponsored jointly with the Center for Middle Eastern Studies), 1962. Harvard University Press.
Communist China 1955–1959: Policy Documents with Analysis, with a foreword by Robert R. Bowie and John K. Fairbank (sponsored jointly with the East Asian Research Center), 1962. Harvard University Press.
Somali Nationalism, by Saadia Touval, 1963. Harvard University Press.
The Dilemma of Mexico's Development, by Raymond Vernon, 1963. Harvard University Press.
Limited War in the Nuclear Age, by Morton H. Halperin, 1963. John Wiley & Sons.
The Arms Debate, by Robert A. Levine, 1963. Harvard University Press.
Africans on the Land, by Montague Yudelman, 1964. Harvard University Press.
Counterinsurgency Warfare, by David Galula, 1964. Frederick A. Praeger, Inc.
People and Policy in the Middle East, by Max Weston Thornburg, 1964. W. W. Norton & Co.
Shaping the Future, by Robert R. Bowie, 1964. Columbia University Press.
Foreign Aid and Foreign Policy, by Edward S. Mason (sponsored jointly with the Council on Foreign Relations), 1964. Harper & Row.
How Nations Negotiate, by Fred Charles Iklé, 1964. Harper & Row.
China and the Bomb, by Morton H. Halperin (sponsored jointly with the East Asian Research Center), 1965. Frederick A. Praeger, Inc.
Democracy in Germany, by Fritz Erler (Jodidi Lectures), 1965. Harvard University Press.
The Troubled Partnership, by Henry A. Kissinger (sponsored jointly with the Council on Foreign Relations), 1965. McGraw-Hill Book Co.
The Rise of Nationalism in Central Africa, by Robert I. Rotberg, 1965. Harvard University Press.
Pan-Africanism and East African Integration, by Joseph S. Nye, Jr., 1965. Harvard University Press.
Communist China and Arms Control, by Morton H. Halperin and Dwight H. Perkins (sponsored jointly with the East Asian Research Center), 1965. Frederick A. Praeger, Inc.

Problems of National Strategy, ed. Henry Kissinger, 1965. Frederick A. Praeger, Inc.

Deterrence before Hiroshima: The Airpower Background of Modern Strategy, by George H. Quester, 1966. John Wiley & Sons.

Containing the Arms Race, by Jeremy J. Stone, 1966. M.I.T. Press.

Germany and the Atlantic Alliance: The Interaction of Strategy and Politics, by James L. Richardson, 1966. Harvard University Press.

Arms and Influence, by Thomas C. Schelling, 1966. Yale University Press.

Political Change in a West African State, by Martin Kilson, 1966. Harvard University Press.

Planning without Facts: Lessons in Resource Allocation from Nigeria's Development, by Wolfgang F. Stolper, 1966. Harvard University Press.

Export Instability and Economic Development, by Alasdair I. MacBean, 1966. Harvard University Press.

Foreign Policy and Democratic Politics, by Kenneth N. Waltz (sponsored jointly with the Institute of War and Peace Studies, Columbia University), 1967. Little, Brown & Co.

Contemporary Military Strategy, by Morton H. Halperin, 1967. Little, Brown & Co.

Sino-Soviet Relations and Arms Control, ed. Morton H. Halperin (sponsored jointly with the East Asian Research Center), 1967. M.I.T. Press.

Africa and United States Policy, by Rupert Emerson, 1967. Prentice-Hall.

Elites in Latin America, edited by Seymour M. Lipset and Aldo Solari, 1967. Oxford University Press.

Europe's Postwar Growth, by Chares P. Kindleberger, 1967. Harvard University Press.

The Rise and Decline of the Cold War, by Paul Seabury, 1967. Basic Books.

Student Politics, ed. S. M. Lipset, 1967. Basic Books.

Pakistan's Development: Social Goals and Private Incentives, by Gustav F. Papanek, 1967. Harvard University Press.

Strike a Blow and Die: A Narrative of Race Relations in Colonial Africa, by George Simeon Mwase, ed. Robert I. Rotberg, 1967. Harvard University Press.

Party Systems and Voter Alignments, edited by Seymour M. Lipset and Stein Rokkan, 1967. Free Press.

Agrarian Socialism, by Seymour M. Lipset, revised edition, 1968. Doubleday Anchor.

Aid, Influence, and Foreign Policy, by Joan M. Nelson, 1968. The Macmillan Company.

International Regionalism, by Joseph S. Nye, 1968. Little, Brown & Co.

Revolution and Counterrevolution, by Seymour M. Lipset, 1968. Basic Books.

Political Order in Changing Societies, by Samuel P. Huntington, 1968. Yale University Press.

The TFX Decision: McNamara and the Military, by Robert J. Art, 1968. Little, Brown & Co.

Korea: The Politics of the Vortex, by Gregory Henderson, 1968. Harvard University Press.

Political Development in Latin America, by Martin Needler, 1968. Random House.

The Precarious Republic, by Michael Hudson, 1968. Random House.
The Brazilian Capital Goods Industry, 1929–1964 (sponsored jointly with the Center for Studies in Education and Development), by Nathaniel H. Leff, 1968. Harvard University Press.
Economic Policy-Making and Development in Brazil, 1947–1964, by Nathaniel H. Leff, 1968. John Wiley & Sons.
Turmoil and Transition: Higher Education and Student Politics in India, edited by Philip G. Altbach, 1968. Lalvani Publishing House (Bombay).
German Foreign Policy in Transition, by Karl Kaiser, 1968. Oxford University Press.
Protest and Power in Black Africa, edited by Robert I. Rotberg, 1969. Oxford University Press.
Peace in Europe, by Karl E. Birnbaum, 1969. Oxford University Press.
The Process of Modernization: An Annotated Bibliography on the Sociocultured Aspects of Development, by John Brode, 1969. Harvard University Press.
Students in Revolt, edited by Seymour M. Lipset and Philip G. Altbach, 1969. Houghton Mifflin.
Agricultural Development in India's Districts: The Intensive Agricultural Districts Programme, by Dorris D. Brown, 1970.
Authoritarian Politics in Modern Society: The Dynamics of Established One-Party Systems, edited by Samuel P. Huntington and Clement H. Moore, 1970. Basic Books.
Nuclear Diplomacy, by George H. Quester, 1970. Dunellen.
The Logic of Images in International Relations, by Robert Jervis, 1970. Princeton University Press.
Europe's Would-Be Polity, by Leon Lindberg and Stuart A. Scheingold, 1970. Prentice-Hall.
Taxation and Development: Lessons from Colombian Experience, by Richard M. Bird, 1970. Harvard University Press.
Lord and Peasant in Peru: A Paradigm of Political and Social Change, by F. LaMond Tullis, 1970. Harvard University Press.
The Kennedy Round in American Trade Policy: The Twilight of the GATT? by John W. Evans, 1971. Harvard University Press.
Korean Development: The Interplay of Politics and Economics, by David C. Cole and Princeton N. Lyman, 1971. Harvard University Press.
Development Policy II — The Pakistan Experience, edited by Walter P. Falcon and Gustav F. Papanek, 1971. Harvard University Press.
Higher Education in a Transitional Society, by Philip G. Altbach, 1971. Sindhu Publications (Bombay).
Studies in Development Planning, edited by Hollis B. Chenery, 1971. Harvard University Press.
Passion and Politics, by Seymour M. Lipset with Gerald Schaflander, 1971. Little, Brown & Co.
Political Mobilization of the Venezuelan Peasant, by John D. Powell, 1971. Harvard University Press.
Higher Education in India, edited by Amrik Singh and Philip Altbach, 1971. Oxford University Press (Delhi).
The Myth of the Guerrilla, by J. Bowyer Bell, 1971. Blond (London) and Knopf (New York).

International Norms and War between States: Three Studies in International Politics, by Kjell Goldmann, 1971. Published jointly by Läromedelsförlagen (Sweden) and the Swedish Institute of International Affairs.

Peace in Parts: Integration and Conflict in Regional Organization, by Joseph S. Nye, Jr., 1971. Little, Brown & Co.

Sovereignty at Bay: The Multinational Spread of U.S. Enterprise, by Raymond Vernon, 1971. Basic Books.

Defense Strategy for the Seventies (revision of *Contemporary Military Strategy*), by Morton H. Halperin, 1971. Little, Brown & Co.

Peasants Against Politics: Rural Organization in Brittany, 1911–1967, by Suzanne Berger, 1972. Harvard University Press.

Transnational Relations and World Politics, edited by Robert O. Keohane and Joseph S. Nye, Jr., 1972. Harvard University Press.

Latin American University Students: A Six Nation Study, by Arthur Liebman, Kenneth N. Walker, and Myron Glazer, 1972. Harvard University Press.

The Politics of Land Reform in Chile, 1950–1970: Public Policy, Political Institutions, and Social Change, by Robert R. Kaufman, 1972. Harvard University Press.

The Boundary Politics of Independent Africa, by Saadia Touval, 1972. Harvard University Press.

The Politics of Nonviolent Action, by Gene E. Sharp, 1973. Porter Sargent.

System 37 Viggen: Arms, Technology, and the Domestication of Glory, by Ingemar Dörfer, 1973. Universitetsforlaget (Oslo).

University Students and African Politics, by William John Hanna, 1974. Africana Publishing Company.

From Cartel to Concorde: Organizing Transnational Enterprise in Advanced Technology, by M. S. Hochmuth, 1974. Sijthoff (Leiden).

Becoming Modern, by Alex Inkeles and David H. Smith, 1974. Harvard University Press.

Economic Nationalism and the Politics of International Dependence: The Case of Copper in Chile, 1945–1973, by Theodore Moran, 1974. Princeton University Press.

The Andean Group: A Case Study in Economic Integration among Developing Countries, by David Morawetz, 1974. M.I.T. Press.

Kenya: The Politics of Participation and Control, by Henry Bienen, 1974. Princeton University Press.

Land Reform and Politics: A Comparative Analysis, by Hung-chao Tai, 1974. University of California Press.

Harvard Studies in International Affairs *
(*formerly Occasional Papers in International Affairs*)

† 1. *A Plan for Planning: The Need for a Better Method of Assisting Underdeveloped Countries on Their Economic Policies*, by Gustav F. Papanek, 1961.
† 2. *The Flow of Resources from Rich to Poor*, by Alan D. Neale, 1961.
† 3. *Limited War: An Essay on the Development of the Theory and an Annotated Bibliography*, by Morton H. Halperin, 1962.
† 4. *Reflections on the Failure of the First West Indian Federation*, by Hugh W. Springer, 1962.
 5. *On the Interaction of Opposing Forces under Possible Arms Agreements*, by Glenn A. Kent, 1963. 36 pp. $1.25.
† 6. *Europe's Northern Cap and the Soviet Union*, by Nils Örvik, 1963.
 7. *Civil Administration in the Punjab: An Analysis of a State Government in India*, by E. N. Mangat Rai, 1963. 82 pp. $1.75.
 8. *On the Appropriate Size of a Development Program*, by Edward S. Mason, 1964. 24 pp. $1.00.
 9. *Self-Determination Revisited in the Era of Decolonization*, by Rupert Emerson, 1964. 64 pp. $1.75.
 10. *The Planning and Execution of Economic Development in Southeast Asia*, by Clair Wilcox, 1965. 37 pp. $1.25.
 11. *Pan-Africanism in Action*, by Albert Tevoedjre, 1965. 88 pp. $2.50.
 12. *Is China Turning In?* by Morton Halperin, 1965. 34 pp. $1.25.
†13. *Economic Development in India and Pakistan*, by Edward S. Mason, 1966.
 14. *The Role of the Military in Recent Turkish Politics*, by Ergun Özbudun, 1966. 54 pp. $1.75.
†15. *Economic Development and Individual Change: A Social-Psychological Study of the Comilla Experiment in Pakistan*, by Howard Schuman, 1967.
 16. *A Select Bibliography on Students, Politics, and Higher Education*, by Philip G. Altbach, UMHE Revised Edition, 1970. 65 pp. $2.75.
 17. *Europe's Political Puzzle: A Study of the Fouchet Negotiations and the 1963 Veto*, by Alessandro Silj, 1967. 178 pp. $3.50.
 18. *The Cap and the Straits: Problems of Nordic Security*, by Jan Klenberg, 1968. 19 pp. $1.25.
 19. *Cyprus: The Law and Politics of Civil Strife*, by Linda B. Miller, 1968. 97 pp. $3.00.
†20. *East and West Pakistan: A Problem in the Political Economy of Regional Planning*, by Md. Anisur Rahman, 1968.
†21. *Internal War and International Systems: Perspectives on Method*, by George A. Kelley and Linda B. Miller, 1969.
†22. *Migrants, Urban Poverty, and Instability in Developing Nations*, by Joan M. Nelson, 1969. 81 pp.

* Available from Harvard University Center for International Affairs, 6 Divinity Avenue, Cambridge, Massachusetts 02138
† Out of print. May be ordered from AMS Press, Inc., 56 East 13th Street, New York, N.Y. 10003

23. *Growth and Development in Pakistan, 1955–1969*, by Joseph J. Stern and Walter P. Falcon, 1970. 94 pp. $3.00.
24. *Higher Education in Developing Countries: A Select Bibliography*, by Philip G. Altbach, 1970. 118 pp. $4.00.
25. *Anatomy of Political Institutionalization: The Case of Israel and Some Comparative Analyses*, by Amos Perlmutter, 1970. 60 pp. $2.50.
†26. *The German Democratic Republic from the Sixties to the Seventies*, by Peter Christian Ludz, 1970. 100 pp.
27. *The Law in Political Integration: The Evolution and Integrative Implications of Regional Legal Processes in the European Community*, by Stuart A. Scheingold, 1971. 63 pp. $2.50.
28. *Psychological Dimensions of U.S.-Japanese Relations*, by Hiroshi Kitamura, 1971. 46 pp. $2.00.
29. *Conflict Regulation in Divided Societies,* by Eric A. Nordlinger, 1972. 137 pp. $4.25.
30. *Israel's Political-Military Doctrine*, by Michael I. Handel, 1973. 101 pp. $3.25.
31. *Italy, NATO, and the European Community: The Interplay of Foreign Policy and Domestic Politics*, by Primo Vannicelli, 1974.
32. *Choice of Technology in Developing Countries*, by C. Peter Timmer, John W. Thomas, Louis T. Wells, Jr., and David Morawetz, 1974.
33. *The International Role of the Communist Parties in France and Italy*, by Donald L. M. Blackmer and Annie Kriegel, 1974.
34. *The Hazards of Peace: A European View of Detente*, by Juan Cassiers, 1974.